CALEB ROSS

C#9 Clean architecture with .NET 5

Copyright © 2024 by Caleb Ross

All rights reserved. No part of this publication may be reproduced, stored or transmitted in any form or by any means, electronic, mechanical, photocopying, recording, scanning, or otherwise without written permission from the publisher. It is illegal to copy this book, post it to a website, or distribute it by any other means without permission.

First edition

This book was professionally typeset on Reedsy.
Find out more at reedsy.com

Contents

Introduction Overview of Clean Architecture	1
Chapter 1: Understanding Clean Architecture	10
Chapter 2: Getting Started with .NET 5 and C#9	19
Chapter 3: Structuring Your Solution for Clean Architecture	29
Chapter 4: Implementing the Domain Layer	45
Chapter 5: Building the Application Layer	57
Chapter 6: Implementing the Infrastructure Layer	71
Chapter 7: Building the User Interface Layer	85
Chapter 8: Testing Strategies in Clean Architecture	99
Chapter 9: Deployment Strategies in Clean Architecture	111
Chapter 10: Security in Clean Architecture	122
Chapter 11: Performance Optimization in Clean Architecture	135
Chapter 12: Advanced Topics in Clean Architecture	146
Chapter 13: Case Studies and Real-World Applications of...	156
Chapter 14: Future Trends in Clean Architecture	163
Chapter 15: Implementing Clean Architecture in Real-World...	172
Conclusion	188

Introduction Overview of Clean Architecture

In software development, the concept of "architecture" refers to the high-level structure of a software system. It involves designing the system's components and their interactions, ensuring that the system is not only functional but also flexible, maintainable, and scalable over time. Among the various architectural patterns available today, Clean Architecture, proposed by Robert C. Martin (commonly known as "Uncle Bob"), has gained significant attention due to its focus on achieving separation of concerns and its clear, modular structure. Clean Architecture provides guidelines on how to build software systems that are easy to understand, test, and maintain while ensuring minimal coupling between components.

At its core, Clean Architecture emphasizes the need for a system to be adaptable to changing requirements without excessive refactoring or rewriting. The guiding principle behind Clean Architecture is that an application's business logic should remain isolated from external systems like databases, frameworks, or user interfaces. By ensuring this isolation, Clean Architecture helps prevent the core of the system from being heavily dependent on infrastructure concerns, making it easier to evolve and maintain over time.

Clean Architecture is not just a rigid, prescriptive pattern; it is a philosophy that encourages thinking deeply about the relationships between components and how dependencies flow within an application. It provides developers with the mental model to organize code into distinct layers with clear boundaries, ensuring that changes in one layer do not ripple unexpectedly through the entire system.

Key Principles of Clean Architecture

- **Separation of Concerns**: Each layer of the architecture has a specific role and responsibility, ensuring that changes in one layer do not affect others unnecessarily.
- **Independence from Frameworks**: The core business logic is isolated from any specific framework or third-party tools, allowing for flexibility in changing technologies.
- **Testability**: The separation of concerns makes it easier to write unit tests and integration tests for the core business logic without needing to mock out infrastructure concerns.
- **Ease of Maintenance**: Clean Architecture promotes code that is easy to read, understand, and maintain over time, reducing technical debt.
- **Dependency Inversion**: High-level modules (business logic) should not depend on low-level modules (infrastructure); rather, both should depend on abstractions. This allows the application to evolve without being tightly coupled to any specific technology.

By adhering to these principles, Clean Architecture enables software systems to remain agile and adaptable as they grow in complexity. It provides a robust foundation that helps ensure code quality, maintainability, and scalability.

Why Clean Architecture Matters in Modern Software Development

In the current landscape of software development, the ability to rapidly evolve and scale applications is paramount. Businesses are constantly adapting to new challenges and opportunities, and software systems must be flexible enough to keep up with these changes. Unfortunately, as applications grow in size and complexity, they often become brittle, difficult to modify, and prone to bugs. This is where Clean Architecture becomes invaluable.

One of the main reasons Clean Architecture is crucial in modern software development is its focus on **flexibility**. As systems evolve, new features are added, and existing functionality is modified. Without a well-structured architecture, these changes can lead to code that becomes tightly coupled, making it harder to introduce new features without inadvertently breaking existing ones. Clean Architecture helps developers avoid this problem by enforcing strict boundaries between different parts of the system. Changes in one part of the system, such as the user interface, do not affect the core business logic, allowing for greater flexibility in adapting to new requirements.

Scalability is another critical factor in modern software development. As applications grow to serve more users and handle more data, they need to be able to scale efficiently. Clean Architecture, by promoting a clear separation of concerns, ensures that the application's core logic is not intertwined with concerns related to scalability, such as database performance or caching. This allows developers to scale the infrastructure independently of the business logic, making it easier to optimize performance as the system grows.

In addition, **maintainability** is a key consideration in the lifecycle of a software project. Over time, the cost of maintaining an application can far exceed the cost of its initial development. Clean Architecture helps mitigate this issue by promoting code that is easy to understand and modify. The clear separation between layers makes it easier to track down bugs and implement new features without introducing unexpected side effects.

Testability is another reason why Clean Architecture matters. In modern development, automated testing is a critical practice for ensuring software quality. By structuring the application in a way that separates business logic from external dependencies, Clean Architecture makes it easier to write unit tests and integration tests. This is particularly important in an era where continuous integration and continuous delivery (CI/CD) pipelines are becoming the standard for software development.

Finally, **technology independence** is a crucial aspect of Clean Architecture. In the fast-moving world of technology, frameworks, libraries, and tools come and go. Clean Architecture allows developers to build applications that are not tied to any specific technology, making it easier to adopt new tools and frameworks as they become available. This flexibility ensures that the application remains relevant and maintainable over the long term.

The Importance of Maintainable and Scalable Code

In software development, maintainability and scalability are two of the most important attributes of a successful system. However, these concepts are often neglected during the initial phases of development, leading to problems as the system grows and evolves.

Maintainability refers to the ease with which a software system can be modified to correct faults, improve performance, or adapt to new requirements. In a maintainable system, changes can be made with minimal effort and without introducing new bugs. One of the key challenges in achieving maintainability is avoiding "spaghetti code," where different parts of the system are tightly coupled and difficult to change in isolation.

Clean Architecture promotes maintainability by enforcing a strict separation between the different layers of the system. Each layer has its own responsibilities and interacts with other layers through well-defined interfaces. This makes it easier to modify one part of the system without affecting the rest, reducing the likelihood of introducing bugs during the modification process.

For example, if a developer needs to update the way data is stored in the database, they can make the necessary changes in the infrastructure layer without touching the business logic or the user interface. This isolation of concerns not only makes the code easier to maintain but also reduces the risk of unexpected side effects.

Scalability, on the other hand, refers to the system's ability to handle an increasing number of users, transactions, or data without a significant decrease in performance. As businesses grow, their software systems need to scale to handle the increased load. Without proper scalability, a system may become slow, unresponsive, or even crash under heavy load.

One of the key challenges in achieving scalability is ensuring that different parts of the system can scale independently. Clean Architecture helps in this regard by isolating the core business logic from concerns related to scalability. For example, the infrastructure layer can be optimized for performance, such

INTRODUCTION OVERVIEW OF CLEAN ARCHITECTURE

as by adding caching or scaling the database, without requiring changes to the core business logic. This separation allows developers to focus on optimizing the parts of the system that need to scale without compromising the overall architecture.

In addition, Clean Architecture promotes **modularity**, which is an essential aspect of scalability. By breaking the system into modular components, each of which can be developed, tested, and scaled independently, Clean Architecture makes it easier to scale the system horizontally. For example, in a microservices architecture, each service can be scaled independently based on its specific needs.

In summary, maintainable and scalable code is critical for the long-term success of any software project. Clean Architecture provides the guidelines and principles necessary to achieve these attributes, ensuring that the system can grow and evolve without becoming unmanageable.

Key Concepts of C#9 and .NET 5

The release of C#9 and .NET 5 brought significant new features and improvements that are particularly relevant to developers building applications using Clean Architecture. By leveraging these features, developers can write cleaner, more expressive code while taking advantage of the performance and scalability improvements provided by .NET 5.

1. C#9 Record Types One of the most exciting new features in C#9 is the introduction of **record types**. Records provide a way to define immutable data structures in a concise and expressive manner. In Clean Architecture, records are particularly useful for defining value objects in the domain layer, which are often immutable and represent concepts like currency, measurements, or other business rules.

For example, consider a value object representing a Money type:

```
csharp
Copy code
public record Money(decimal Amount, string Currency);
```

This simple declaration creates a value object that is immutable and provides built-in functionality for equality comparison, making it ideal for use in Clean Architecture's domain layer.

2. C#9 Init-Only Setters Another useful feature introduced in C#9 is **init-only setters**. These allow properties to be initialized at object creation but prevent further modification, which is useful for creating immutable objects. This is particularly important in Clean Architecture, where immutability helps prevent unintended side effects and makes the system easier to reason about.

For example, an entity in the domain layer might use init-only properties to ensure that its state cannot be changed after creation:

```csharp
Copy code
public class Customer
{
    public string FirstName { get; init; }
    public string LastName { get; init; }
}
```

This ensures that the Customer object's properties are only set once, at the time of creation, and cannot be modified later.

3. Pattern Matching Enhancements C#9 also introduced several enhancements to **pattern matching**, making it easier to write expressive and concise code. Pattern matching is useful in Clean Architecture for implementing business logic in a way that is both clear and maintainable.

For example, pattern matching can be used in the application layer to handle different types of commands or queries:

```csharp
Copy code
public string GetCustomerStatus(Customer customer) => customer switch
{
    { IsPremium
```

: true } => "Premium Customer", { IsPremium: false } => "Regular Customer",
_ => "Unknown Customer" };

```vbnet
Copy code
```

These enhancements make it easier to implement business logic in a clean, readable manner without introducing unnecessary complexity.

4. .NET 5 Performance Improvements
.NET 5 brought significant performance improvements, particularly in the areas of Just-In-Time (JIT) compilation, garbage collection, and asynchronous programming. These improvements are particularly important for developers building scalable applications with Clean Architecture, as they help ensure that the system remains performant even as it scales.

For example, .NET 5 includes optimizations for asynchronous programming, which is often used in Clean Architecture to handle long-running tasks, such as database queries or external API calls, without blocking the main thread.

5. Cross-Platform Development
One of the key goals of .NET 5 is to unify the .NET ecosystem, providing a single platform for building applications that run on Windows, macOS, and Linux. This cross-platform capability is particularly important for developers using Clean Architecture, as it ensures that their applications can run in a variety of environments without requiring significant changes to the codebase.

By leveraging the cross-platform capabilities of .NET 5, developers can build applications that are portable and can be deployed on a variety of platforms, including cloud environments, on-premises servers, and edge devices.

How to Use This Book

This book is designed to be a comprehensive guide to building scalable and maintainable applications using C#9, .NET 5, and Clean Architecture principles. Whether you are a beginner looking to learn the basics of Clean Architecture or an experienced developer looking to refine your skills, this book has something to offer.

The book is organized into chapters that build on each other, starting with the foundational concepts of Clean Architecture and progressing to more advanced topics, such as performance optimization, testing, and cloud deployment. Each chapter includes practical examples and code samples to help you understand the concepts being discussed.

Here's how you can get the most out of this book:

1. **Follow the Chapters Sequentially**: The book is structured in a way that each chapter builds on the knowledge gained in the previous chapters. While it is possible to jump to specific chapters, you will get the most benefit by reading the book in order.

2. **Work Through the Code Samples**: The best way to learn is by doing. Each chapter includes code samples and exercises that will help you apply the concepts discussed in the chapter. Take the time to work through these examples and try implementing them in your own projects.

3. **Use the Book as a Reference**: As you work on your own projects, you can refer back to the book to refresh your memory on specific concepts or best practices. The book is designed to be a practical reference that you can use throughout your career as a software developer.

4. **Engage with the Community**: Clean Architecture is a broad and evolving topic, and there is always more to learn. Consider joining online communities, such as forums or social media groups, where you can discuss Clean Architecture, share your experiences, and learn from others.

By the end of this book, you will have a solid understanding of Clean Architecture principles and how to apply them using C#9 and .NET 5. You will be equipped with the knowledge and skills to

INTRODUCTION OVERVIEW OF CLEAN ARCHITECTURE

build scalable, maintainable applications that stand the test of time.

This introduction provides a comprehensive foundation for your readers, setting the stage for t

Chapter 1: Understanding Clean Architecture

The Origins of Clean Architecture

Clean Architecture, as the name suggests, is about structuring software in a way that makes it clean—both in its implementation and in the interactions between various parts of the system. The concept was proposed by Robert C. Martin, commonly referred to as "Uncle Bob," in a blog post he published in 2012. However, the roots of Clean Architecture trace back to earlier architectural patterns like Hexagonal Architecture (also known as Ports and Adapters) by Alistair Cockburn and the Onion Architecture popularized by Jeffrey Palermo. All of these patterns share the goal of creating a system that is decoupled, flexible, testable, and maintainable. They emphasize separating concerns by decoupling core business logic from external systems, like databases, user interfaces, or third-party services.

Clean Architecture aims to improve upon these earlier patterns by providing more structure and clearer guidelines for organizing code. It draws from several established principles in software development, including the **Single Responsibility Principle (SRP)**, **Dependency Inversion Principle (DIP)**, and **Open-Closed Principle (OCP)** from SOLID programming. At the core of Clean Architecture is the idea that the inner layers (business rules, domain logic) should not depend on the outer layers (UI, frameworks, or databases).

Instead, the dependencies should flow inwards, towards the more abstract business logic.

The motivation behind Clean Architecture was to address the problems that arise in large-scale software systems, particularly the issue of **tight coupling**. As software systems evolve, they tend to become increasingly difficult to change. Adding new features often requires extensive refactoring, and changes in one part of the system can have unintended side effects elsewhere. Clean Architecture provides a framework for organizing code in a way that minimizes these risks by enforcing strict boundaries between different parts of the system.

In the context of **C#9 and .NET 5**, Clean Architecture allows developers to write applications that are not only scalable and maintainable but also portable across different frameworks and platforms. This architecture fits well with modern software development practices, such as microservices, cloud computing, and DevOps, as it helps ensure that the core business logic is independent of the specific technologies used to implement it.

Key Principles: Independence of Frameworks, UI, and Databases

One of the most important principles of Clean Architecture is that the **core business logic** should be completely independent of external concerns such as frameworks, databases, or user interfaces. This independence is achieved by enforcing **separation of concerns**, which means that each layer of the architecture has a specific role and responsibility.

Let's break down these key principles:

1. **Independence of Frameworks**

In many applications, the choice of framework tends to dictate how the application is structured. However, in Clean Architecture, the framework is treated as a **plugin** to the application, rather than something that dictates its structure. The core business logic is written in such a way that it does not depend on any specific framework. This allows developers to swap out frameworks or update to newer versions without needing to make changes to the core logic.

For example, in a typical ASP.NET Core application, the framework provides features like dependency injection, routing, and middleware. In a

Clean Architecture application, these features are used in the outer layers of the architecture, but the core business logic is completely unaware of the framework. The application could just as easily be implemented with another framework, such as Blazor or Xamarin, without requiring any changes to the core logic.

2. **Independence of User Interface (UI)**

In many traditional applications, the user interface is tightly coupled to the business logic. This makes it difficult to change the UI without affecting the underlying logic. In Clean Architecture, the UI is treated as just another interface to the system. The core business logic is completely independent of the UI, allowing the UI to be changed or replaced without affecting the rest of the system.

For example, a Clean Architecture application might have a web-based UI, a mobile app UI, and a desktop UI, all of which interact with the same core business logic. The key is that the business logic is agnostic to how it is being presented to the user. This makes it easier to support multiple platforms or update the UI without requiring changes to the core application.

3. **Independence of Databases**

One of the most common sources of tight coupling in traditional architectures is the database. Many applications are structured in such a way that the business logic is tightly coupled to the specific database being used, which makes it difficult to change the database or move to a different storage system.

In Clean Architecture, the database is treated as an **implementation detail** rather than a core part of the system. The core business logic interacts with the database through well-defined interfaces (often referred to as repositories), but it is completely unaware of the specific database technology being used. This allows the database to be swapped out or replaced without requiring changes to the business logic.

For example, in a Clean Architecture application, the core logic might interact with an interface like IRepository<T>, which abstracts away the details of how data is stored. The actual implementation of this interface might use a SQL database, a NoSQL database, or even an in-memory data store, but the core logic remains unchanged regardless of the underlying storage system.

Layers and Boundaries: Domain, Application, and Infrastructure

At the heart of Clean Architecture is the concept of **layers** and **boundaries**. Each layer of the architecture has a specific role and responsibility, and the layers interact with each other through well-defined interfaces. The key layers in Clean Architecture are the **Domain Layer**, the **Application Layer**, and the **Infrastructure Layer**. In some implementations, there may also be additional layers, such as the **UI Layer** or the **Presentation Layer**.

Let's explore each of these layers in detail:

1. **Domain Layer**

The **Domain Layer** is the core of the system. It contains the business logic and the rules that govern how the system behaves. The Domain Layer is completely independent of any external systems, including the UI, the database, and any third-party libraries. This makes it the most important layer in the architecture, as it represents the core functionality of the system.

In the Domain Layer, you'll typically find the following components:

- **Entities**: These are the objects that represent the core concepts in the system. Entities typically have an identity and encapsulate business rules. For example, in an e-commerce system, an Order might be an entity that has a collection of OrderLine items and rules for calculating the total cost.
- **Value Objects**: These are objects that represent concepts with no identity, such as money, measurements, or dates. Value objects are often immutable and can be used to enforce business rules. For example, a Money value object might ensure that a valid currency is always specified.
- **Domain Services**: These are services that encapsulate business logic that doesn't naturally belong to any specific entity. For example, a PaymentService might handle the process of charging a customer's credit card.
- **Aggregates**: Aggregates are groups of entities that are treated as a single unit. They ensure consistency and encapsulate business rules that span multiple entities. For example, an Order might be an aggregate that contains OrderLine items and ensures that the total price is always

calculated correctly.

The Domain Layer is completely independent of any external concerns, such as the database or the UI. This means that it can be tested in isolation, without needing to mock out infrastructure components.

2. **Application Layer**

The **Application Layer** is responsible for orchestrating the flow of data between the Domain Layer and the external systems, such as the UI or the database. It contains the **use cases** that define how the system behaves in response to specific inputs.

In the Application Layer, you'll typically find the following components:

- **Use Cases**: These are the specific actions that the system can perform. For example, a use case might be "Place an Order" or "Charge a Customer." Each use case interacts with the Domain Layer to perform business logic and with the Infrastructure Layer to persist data or send notifications.
- **Command Handlers**: These handle specific commands (e.g., "CreateOrderCommand") and execute the corresponding use case.
- **Query Handlers**: These handle queries (e.g., "GetCustomerDetailsQuery") and retrieve data from the system.
- **Services**: Application services may interact with the Domain Layer, coordinating actions like processing a payment or managing user authentication.

The Application Layer is where the business rules defined in the Domain Layer are applied to specific use cases. It is also responsible for interacting with external systems, such as databases or message queues, through well-defined interfaces.

3. **Infrastructure Layer**

The **Infrastructure Layer** is responsible for handling the external concerns of the system, such as databases, file storage, or external APIs. This is where the actual implementations of the repositories and services that the Domain and Application layers depend on are located.

CHAPTER 1: UNDERSTANDING CLEAN ARCHITECTURE

In the Infrastructure Layer, you'll typically find the following components:

- **Repositories**: These are the concrete implementations of the repository interfaces defined in the Application Layer. For example, a SqlCustom erRepository might interact with a SQL database to retrieve and store customer data.
- **Data Access**: This is where the actual interaction with the database occurs, whether it's through Entity Framework Core, Dapper, or raw SQL.
- **External Services**: These are the integrations with third-party services, such as payment gateways, email providers, or external APIs.
- **Infrastructure Services**: These are services related to logging, caching, and other cross-cutting concerns.

The key to the Infrastructure Layer is that it should be completely interchangeable. The core business logic in the Domain Layer doesn't know or care how data is persisted or how external services are called—it only interacts with interfaces defined in the Application Layer.

The Role of Dependency Injection

Dependency Injection (DI) is a fundamental concept in Clean Architecture, and it plays a key role in decoupling different layers of the system. The idea behind DI is that instead of a class directly instantiating its dependencies, it receives them through its constructor or a method parameter. This decoupling allows for greater flexibility and easier testing, as different implementations of a dependency can be swapped out without modifying the dependent class.

In Clean Architecture, DI is typically used to inject the concrete implementations of services, repositories, and other dependencies from the Infrastructure Layer into the Application Layer. This is usually done in the composition root, which is the entry point of the application, such as the Startup class in an ASP.NET Core application.

Here's an example of how DI might be used in a Clean Architecture application:

```csharp
Copy code
public class OrderService
{
    private readonly IOrderRepository _orderRepository;
    private readonly IPaymentGateway _paymentGateway;

    public OrderService(IOrderRepository orderRepository,
    IPaymentGateway paymentGateway)
    {
        _orderRepository = orderRepository;
        _paymentGateway = paymentGateway;
    }

    public void PlaceOrder(Order order)
    {
        _orderRepository.Save(order);
        _paymentGateway.ProcessPayment(order.Total);
    }
}
```

In this example, the OrderService depends on an IOrderRepository and an IPaymentGateway, but it doesn't know or care about the concrete implementations of these interfaces. At runtime, the application will inject the appropriate implementations, such as SqlOrderRepository and StripePaymentGateway.

DI is especially important in Clean Architecture because it allows for **inversion of control** (IoC), where the flow of dependencies is inverted. Instead of high-level modules (e.g., the Domain Layer) depending on low-level modules (e.g., the Infrastructure Layer), both depend on abstractions. This makes it easier to swap out dependencies, write unit tests, and ensure that the application remains flexible and maintainable over time.

Comparing Clean Architecture to Other Patterns (e.g., N-Tier, Onion)

While Clean Architecture is a powerful pattern for organizing code, it's not the only architectural pattern available. Several other patterns, such as the **N-Tier Architecture** and **Onion Architecture**, share similar goals but differ

CHAPTER 1: UNDERSTANDING CLEAN ARCHITECTURE

in their implementation and focus. Let's compare Clean Architecture with these patterns to understand how they differ and why Clean Architecture might be a better fit for certain applications.

1. **N-Tier Architecture**

N-Tier Architecture is one of the oldest and most widely used architectural patterns. It divides the system into separate layers, such as the presentation layer (UI), the business logic layer, and the data access layer. Each layer is responsible for a specific concern, and the layers interact with each other in a top-down manner. For example, the presentation layer interacts with the business logic layer, and the business logic layer interacts with the data access layer.

While N-Tier Architecture shares some similarities with Clean Architecture, there are several key differences:

- In N-Tier Architecture, the dependencies typically flow **downwards**, from the presentation layer to the data access layer. This means that the business logic layer often depends on the data access layer, which can lead to tight coupling.
- In Clean Architecture, the dependencies flow **inwards**, towards the core business logic. The business logic does not depend on the data access layer or the UI, making it more flexible and easier to test.
- N-Tier Architecture is often criticized for its lack of clear boundaries between the layers. In many implementations, the business logic ends up being spread across multiple layers, making it harder to maintain and test.

In contrast, Clean Architecture enforces strict boundaries between the different layers, ensuring that the core business logic is isolated from external concerns.

2. **Onion Architecture**

Onion Architecture, proposed by Jeffrey Palermo, is another architectural pattern that shares many similarities with Clean Architecture. Both patterns emphasize the importance of separating concerns and decoupling the core business logic from external systems.

The key difference between Onion Architecture and Clean Architecture is the way they structure the layers. In Onion Architecture, the layers are arranged in a series of concentric rings, with the core domain model at the center. Each layer depends on the layers closer to the center, but not on the layers farther out. This is similar to Clean Architecture, where the dependencies flow inwards towards the core business logic.

However, Clean Architecture is more **flexible** in terms of how the layers are structured. While Onion Architecture tends to have a strict hierarchy of layers, Clean Architecture allows for more flexibility in how the layers are organized and how they interact with each other. For example, in Clean Architecture, the application layer can interact with both the domain layer and the infrastructure layer, whereas in Onion Architecture, the layers are typically more strictly separated.

Another difference is that Clean Architecture provides more explicit guidelines for handling **external concerns**, such as databases and UI frameworks. In Onion Architecture, these concerns are often treated as part of the infrastructure layer, whereas in Clean Architecture, they are treated as plugins that can be swapped out without affecting the core business logic.

In conclusion, while both N-Tier and Onion Architectures share some similarities with Clean Architecture, Clean Architecture offers a more **structured** and **flexible** approach to organizing code. By enforcing strict boundaries between the different layers and promoting the use of Dependency Injection and Dependency Inversion, Clean Architecture helps ensure that the system remains maintainable, testable, and adaptable over time.

This chapter provides a deep understanding of Clean Architecture, its principles, and how it compares to other architectural patterns. It sets the stage for the subsequent chapters, where these concepts will be applied in the context of C#9 and .NET 5 to build scalable and maintainable applications.

Chapter 2: Getting Started with .NET 5 and C#9

I ntroduction
- Overview of the chapter's purpose.
- The importance of understanding the .NET 5 ecosystem.
- How C#9 integrates with Clean Architecture.

Setting Up Your Development Environment

- Required tools for .NET 5 and C#9 development.
- Visual Studio / Visual Studio Code setup.
- Installing the .NET 5 SDK.
- Installing necessary extensions or plugins (C# tools, Docker for containerization, etc.).
- Setting up a new project in Visual Studio or Visual Studio Code.
- Creating a new ASP.NET Core Web Application.
- Choosing the right project template (API, Web Application, etc.).
- Structuring the project according to Clean Architecture.
- Initial project configuration.
- Setting up the appsettings.json for configuration management.
- Organizing the folder structure for Clean Architecture: Domain, Appli-

cation, Infrastructure, and UI.

Overview of .NET 5 and Its Features

- The significance of .NET 5 as a unified platform.
- Cross-platform compatibility (Windows, Linux, macOS).
- Unified runtime for desktop, web, mobile, cloud, and IoT applications.
- Performance improvements in .NET 5 (GC, Just-In-Time compilation).
- Why .NET 5 is essential for Clean Architecture.
- Built-in support for Dependency Injection.
- Improved API for asynchronous programming.
- Enhanced tooling for code quality (Roslyn, analyzers).
- Cross-platform advantages for enterprise-level applications.
- Key features and improvements in .NET 5.
- Performance enhancements.
- Single runtime across multiple platforms.
- Native support for Windows Forms, WPF, and Blazor.

Introduction to C#9 Language Enhancements

- What's new in C#9 and why these features are relevant for Clean Architecture.
- Focus on immutability, concise code, and clarity.
- Streamlined syntax for common patterns.

C#9 Record Types

- Understanding record types: Immutable, value-based types.
- Comparison with traditional class structures.
- How record types simplify domain entities and value objects in Clean Architecture.
- Syntax overview:

```csharp
Copy code
public record Person(string FirstName, string LastName);
```

- How to integrate records with domain models.
- Real-world example: Implementing value objects with record types.

Init-Only Setters

- Introduction to init-only setters: Defining immutable properties.
- How init-only setters complement records for immutability.
- Syntax overview:

```csharp
Copy code
public class Person
{
    public string FirstName { get; init; }
    public string LastName { get; init; }
}
```

- Best practices for using init-only setters in the domain layer.
- Example: Applying init-only setters to domain entities in Clean Architecture.

Pattern Matching Enhancements

- Overview of pattern matching in C#9.
- Enhanced pattern matching syntax for switch expressions.
- Syntax overview:

```csharp
Copy code
public string GetPersonDescription(Person person) => person switch
{
    { FirstName: "John" } => "John is here.",
    { FirstName: "Jane" } => "Jane is here.",
    _ => "Unknown person."
};
```

- Applying pattern matching to business logic in the application layer.
- Use cases: Decision-making and handling complex domain scenarios.

Top-Level Programs

- Simplified syntax for entry-point methods with top-level programs.
- Overview of top-level program syntax:

```csharp
Copy code
Console.WriteLine("Hello, World!");
```

- How to leverage top-level programs in small Clean Architecture components or utilities.
- When to use top-level programs for simpler, utility-based services.

With Expressions

- Overview of with expressions in C#9 for creating modified copies of immutable objects.
- Syntax overview:

```csharp
Copy code
var newPerson = person with { LastName = "Smith" };
```

- Use cases in Clean Architecture: Updating value objects immutably.
- Practical example: Modifying domain entities with with-expressions.

Covariant Return Types

- Understanding covariant return types.
- How covariant return types allow more flexibility in inheritance hierarchies.
- Syntax overview and example:

```csharp
Copy code
class Animal
{
    public virtual Animal GetAnimal() => new Animal();
}

class Dog : Animal
{
    public override Dog GetAnimal() => new Dog();
}
```

- Applying covariant return types in the application layer to return specific entities or services.

Creating Your First Clean Architecture Project

- Step-by-step guide to setting up a Clean Architecture project.
- Initializing a new project with .NET 5 and C#9.
- Structuring the project according to Clean Architecture.
- Creating the core layers:
- Domain layer: Entities, value objects, aggregates, and domain services.
- Application layer: Use cases, command handlers, query handlers.
- Infrastructure layer: Repositories, data access, and external services.
- UI layer (optional): Web API setup or MVC for presentation.
- Configuring Dependency Injection.
- Registering services, repositories, and external dependencies in the composition root.
- Example of setting up DI in Startup.cs:

```csharp
Copy code
public void ConfigureServices(IServiceCollection services)
{
    services.AddScoped<IOrderRepository, SqlOrderRepository>();
    services.AddScoped<IPaymentGateway, StripePaymentGateway>();
}
```

Setting Up Dependency Injection in .NET 5

- Deep dive into Dependency Injection (DI) in .NET 5.
- Built-in DI container in ASP.NET Core.
- Scopes: Transient, Scoped, and Singleton.
- Best practices for setting up DI in Clean Architecture.
- Registering dependencies:
- Domain services, application services, infrastructure repositories.
- Example:

```csharp
Copy code
services.AddScoped<IOrderService, OrderService>();
services.AddScoped<ICustomerRepository, CustomerRepository>();
```

- Resolving dependencies in controllers and services.
- How DI promotes separation of concerns in Clean Architecture.

Best Practices for Structuring a Clean Architecture Project

- Key principles for organizing folders and files in Clean Architecture.
- Domain, Application, Infrastructure, and UI folder structure.
- Example of a well-structured project:
- Domain/Entities/Order.cs
- Application/Services/OrderService.cs
- Infrastructure/Data/SqlOrderRepository.cs
- UI/Controllers/OrderController.cs
- How to avoid common pitfalls (e.g., overcomplicating project structure).

Organizing the Folder Structure According to Clean Architecture

- Best practices for organizing the folder structure in a Clean Architecture project.
- Layer-by-layer organization: Domain, Application, Infrastructure, and UI.
- Example folder structure:
- Domain/Entities/Order.cs
- Application/Services/OrderService.cs
- Infrastructure/Data/SqlOrderRepository.cs
- UI/Controllers/OrderController.cs
- How to avoid common mistakes in folder organization.

Configuring Application Settings and Dependencies

- Overview of the appsettings.json file in .NET 5.
- Storing environment-specific configurations.
- Best practices for handling sensitive data (secrets management).
- Example configuration:

```json
Copy code
{
    "ConnectionStrings": {
        "DefaultConnection":
        "Server=myServerAddress;Database=myDataBase;User
        Id=myUsername;Password=myPassword;"
    }
}
```

- Injecting configurations into services using the options pattern:
- Example:

```csharp
Copy code
public class DatabaseSettings
{
    public string ConnectionString { get; set; }
}

public void ConfigureServices
(IServiceCollection services)
{
    services.Configure
<DatabaseSettings>
(Configuration.
GetSection("ConnectionStrings"));
```

}

Building a Simple API with Clean Architecture

- Step-by-step guide to building a basic API using Clean Architecture principles.
- Setting up a simple Web API project in ASP.NET Core.
- Implementing the core layers: Domain, Application, Infrastructure, and UI.
- Creating the Order entity, the OrderService, and the OrderController.
- Step-by-step implementation of a CRUD API for managing orders.
- Example controller setup:

```csharp
Copy code
[ApiController]
[Route("api/[controller]")]
public class OrderController : ControllerBase
{
    private readonly IOrderService _orderService;

    public OrderController
(IOrderService orderService)
    {
        _orderService = orderService;
    }

    [HttpPost]
    public IActionResult CreateOrder
(OrderDto orderDto)
    {
        _orderService.CreateOrder(orderDto);
        return Ok();
    }
}
```

Testing Your Clean Architecture Project

- Importance of testing in Clean Architecture.
- Unit tests for domain and application layers.
- Integration tests for infrastructure and UI layers.
- Setting up unit tests with xUnit or NUnit.
- Writing unit tests for the OrderService.
- Example:

```csharp
Copy code
[Fact]
public void CreateOrder_
ShouldCallRepository()
{
    // Arrange
    var mockRepository = new Mock<
IOrderRepository>();
    var orderService = new OrderService(mockRepository.Object);

    // Act
    orderService.CreateOrder(new Order());

    // Assert
    mockRepository.Verify(r =>
r.Add(It.IsAny<Order>()), Times.Once);
}
```

Final Thoughts and Next Steps

- Recap of key points covered in the chapter.
- Importance of having a clean and well-structured project setup.
- Preparing for more advanced topics like CQRS, performance optimization, and scalability in upcoming chapters.

Chapter 3: Structuring Your Solution for Clean Architecture

Introduction
- Overview of the importance of solution structure.
- Why Clean Architecture relies on clear, organized code structure.
- How following Clean Architecture principles benefits long-term scalability, maintainability, and flexibility in projects.

Designing the Folder Structure

One of the foundational aspects of implementing Clean Architecture is ensuring the codebase is well-organized and follows a logical folder structure. A poorly structured solution will lead to a fragmented understanding of the architecture, making it harder for teams to navigate and maintain the project over time.

Domain Layer Folder Structure

The **Domain Layer** is the core of your application, encapsulating the business rules and the entities that define the system. The domain should be decoupled from external systems, like databases or user interfaces, so it remains isolated from changes in those areas.

A standard folder structure for the Domain Layer may look like this:

```css
Copy code
Domain/
    Entities/
        Order.cs
        Customer.cs
    ValueObjects/
        Money.cs
        Address.cs
    Services/
        OrderService.cs
        PaymentService.cs
    Interfaces/
        IOrderRepository.cs
        IPaymentGateway.cs
```

- **Entities**: This folder holds the core business entities such as Order, Customer, and others. These classes encapsulate the primary business logic related to the data they manage. For example, an Order entity might contain methods to calculate the total price or validate items.
- **ValueObjects**: Value objects are immutable, distinguishable only by their value, not identity. A Money value object, for instance, could represent an amount and currency, ensuring that every operation with monetary values remains consistent and domain-driven.
- **Services**: The Domain Layer services (sometimes called domain services) contain business logic that doesn't naturally belong to any single entity, or that might involve multiple entities. For example, OrderService might handle the rules for placing an order, applying discounts, or validating stock availability.
- **Interfaces**: Defining interfaces within the domain helps abstract out the persistence layer, keeping the domain pure from infrastructure concerns. For example, IOrderRepository is an interface for repositories handling order persistence.

Application Layer Folder Structure

CHAPTER 3: STRUCTURING YOUR SOLUTION FOR CLEAN ARCHITECTURE

The **Application Layer** is responsible for orchestrating the use cases of your application. It acts as the intermediary between the domain logic and the infrastructure. This is where the actual business logic interacts with the repositories, services, and external systems.

A typical Application Layer folder structure:

```markdown
Copy code
Application/
    UseCases/
        PlaceOrder/
            PlaceOrderCommand.cs
            PlaceOrderHandler.cs
    Interfaces/
        IOrderService.cs
    DTOs/
        OrderDto.cs
        CustomerDto.cs
    Exceptions/
        InvalidOrderException.cs
        OrderNotFoundException.cs
```

- **UseCases**: This folder contains specific use cases of your application. For example, PlaceOrder would include commands, handlers, and other related components to execute this use case. Each use case follows the command/query pattern for simplicity and clarity.
- **Interfaces**: These interfaces define contracts for the application services that are implemented in the infrastructure or presentation layers.
- **DTOs (Data Transfer Objects)**: The DTOs represent the data that travels between layers of your system. For example, OrderDto may hold simplified representations of your Order entity meant for API responses or UI purposes.
- **Exceptions**: Custom exceptions specific to the application, such as InvalidOrderException or OrderNotFoundException, encapsulate error cases in a structured, readable way.

Infrastructure Layer Folder Structure

The **Infrastructure Layer** is where you implement the infrastructure-specific details, such as repository classes for database interactions, external API services, and other system dependencies. It is responsible for communicating with external frameworks, APIs, and databases.

A suggested Infrastructure Layer structure:

```markdown
Copy code
Infrastructure/
    Data/
        SqlOrderRepository.cs
        SqlCustomerRepository.cs
    Services/
        StripePaymentGateway.cs
    Logging/
        Logger.cs
```

- **Data**: This folder contains the actual implementation of repositories for interacting with the database. For example, SqlOrderRepository might interact with an SQL database to save and retrieve order data.
- **Services**: Services here are typically those that integrate with external systems, such as payment gateways (e.g., StripePaymentGateway) or messaging services (e.g., EmailService).
- **Logging**: Logging services that capture errors or trace application flow can be encapsulated within the infrastructure layer, providing clean separation of cross-cutting concerns.

UI Layer Folder Structure

The **UI Layer** (User Interface) is where your application interacts with the user or client-facing services. It could be web-based, a mobile UI, or even a command-line interface. This layer is fully decoupled from the business logic and interacts with the application layer via controllers or API endpoints.

A typical structure:

CHAPTER 3: STRUCTURING YOUR SOLUTION FOR CLEAN ARCHITECTURE

```
markdown
Copy code
UI/
    Controllers/
        OrderController.cs
        CustomerController.cs
    Views/
        OrderView.cshtml
        CustomerView.cshtml
    Api/
        OrderApi.cs
```

- **Controllers**: Controllers handle HTTP requests in a web application and delegate tasks to the application layer. For example, OrderController processes requests related to placing, updating, or viewing orders.
- **Views**: If your UI includes a web application with server-side rendering, Views contains HTML or Razor pages that render the user interface.
- **API**: The API folder could hold RESTful APIs that serve data to front-end applications, mobile apps, or external systems. In Clean Architecture, these APIs interact directly with the Application Layer's use cases.

Layering the Application: Domain, Application, Infrastructure, and UI Layers

As we've discussed the folder structure, let's dive into how each layer works and communicates with the others.

1. The Domain Layer

This is the core layer, housing the business rules and logic, and is fully decoupled from any external systems. The Domain Layer's independence makes it easy to test and maintain. The classes here include business logic, value objects, and domain events. Dependencies should always flow **towards** the Domain Layer, and nothing in this layer should depend on external services or frameworks.

2. The Application Layer

The Application Layer is responsible for orchestrating operations. It implements the **use cases** that are defined by the business requirements. For example, if you have an e-commerce system, you might define use cases like "Place Order" or "Cancel Order."

The key responsibilities of the Application Layer include:

- **Handling Commands and Queries**: In Clean Architecture, a command handles actions that change the system's state (e.g., PlaceOrderCommand), while a query retrieves data without changing the state (e.g., GetOrderQuery).
- **Interfacing with Repositories**: The Application Layer interacts with repositories to persist or retrieve domain objects. It ensures that the business logic (from the Domain Layer) is applied correctly to the data retrieved from the database.
- **Interfacing with External Services**: The Application Layer is also responsible for interacting with external services such as payment gateways, messaging services, or external APIs.

3. The Infrastructure Layer

The Infrastructure Layer is where all external systems are integrated. This includes database interactions, API calls, logging, and messaging. It contains the actual implementations for the interfaces defined in the Application Layer. For example, if the Application Layer defines an IOrderRepository, the Infrastructure Layer will implement SqlOrderRepository, which interacts with an SQL database.

The Infrastructure Layer is also responsible for:

- **Data Persistence**: All database operations go through this layer.
- **Service Integration**: External services, like third-party APIs or payment gateways, are integrated here.
- **Cross-Cutting Concerns**: These include logging, error handling, and any other concerns that span across multiple layers.

CHAPTER 3: STRUCTURING YOUR SOLUTION FOR CLEAN ARCHITECTURE

4. The UI Layer

The UI Layer, as mentioned before, interacts with the end-user. This could be a web application, a mobile app, or a desktop app. It communicates with the Application Layer through **controllers** or **presenters**. This layer is also fully decoupled from the Domain Layer, ensuring that the core business logic can be reused across different UIs (e.g., a web app, mobile app, or REST API).

Best Practices for Code Organization and Separation of Concerns

Code organization is critical to maintaining long-term scalability and readability. Here are some best practices:

1. **Keep the Domain Pure**: The Domain Layer should not depend on external systems or frameworks. This allows the core business logic to be reusable and testable.
2. **Use Dependency Injection**: Dependency Injection (DI) ensures loose coupling between layers and helps you manage dependencies in a scalable way. For example, injecting repositories into services ensures that services don't need to instantiate their own dependencies.
3. **Adopt a Command-Query Responsibility Segregation (CQRS) Pattern**: Using separate command and query objects can help simplify logic. Commands change system state, while queries simply retrieve data.
4. **Limit Cross-Layer Dependencies**: Avoid making one layer responsible for tasks that belong to another. For example, UI logic should not call domain logic directly; instead, it should go through the Application Layer.
5. **Avoid Large "God" Classes**: Each class or service should have a clear, single responsibility. If a class grows too large, consider splitting it into smaller, more manageable components.

Creating Interfaces for Loose Coupling

One of the central tenets of Clean Architecture is

40

ChatGPT said:

ChatGPT

to rely heavily on interfaces to promote loose coupling between layers. Here's how to implement this principle effectively:

- **Define Interfaces in the Domain Layer**: While the Domain Layer is typically free of external dependencies, you may define interfaces that represent contracts for repositories, services, or gateways that the application might use.
- **Implement Interfaces in the Infrastructure Layer**: The actual implementations for these interfaces will reside in the Infrastructure Layer, where database or API-specific code lives.
- **Use Dependency Injection**: Register these interfaces in the DI container. For instance:

```csharp
Copy code
public void ConfigureServices(IServiceCollection services)
{
    services.AddScoped<IOrderRepository, SqlOrderRepository>();
    services.AddScoped<IPaymentGateway, StripePaymentGateway>();
}
```

- **Inject Dependencies in Application Services**: This ensures that application services rely on interfaces rather than concrete implementations, allowing for easier testing and flexibility in swapping implementations.

Setting Up a New Clean Architecture Project

Now that you have a solid understanding of the theory behind Clean Architecture, let's set up a practical project using .NET 5 and C#9. Below is a step-by-step guide to create a simple order management system.

Step 1: Create a New ASP.NET Core Project

CHAPTER 3: STRUCTURING YOUR SOLUTION FOR CLEAN ARCHITECTURE

1. Open Visual Studio (or your preferred IDE) and select **Create a new project**.
2. Choose **ASP.NET Core Web Application**.
3. Name your project (e.g., OrderManagementSystem) and choose the location.
4. Select **API** as the project template and ensure that **.NET 5** is selected.

Step 2: Install Required NuGet Packages

Open the NuGet Package Manager Console and run the following commands to install necessary packages:

```bash
Copy code
Install-Package Microsoft.EntityFrameworkCore.SqlServer
Install-Package Microsoft.EntityFrameworkCore.Tools
Install-Package AutoMapper.Extensions.Microsoft.DependencyInjection
Install-Package FluentValidation.AspNetCore
```

Step 3: Set Up the Folder Structure

Within the project, create the necessary folder structure to support Clean Architecture. You can do this manually or use an extension that helps scaffold the structure.

```plaintext
Copy code
OrderManagementSystem/
    Domain/
    Application/
    Infrastructure/
    UI/
```

Step 4: Implement the Domain Layer

- Create entities such as Order and Customer, as well as value objects like Money and Address.

- Define interfaces in the Domain Layer for repositories that will be implemented in the Infrastructure Layer.

Example Order.cs:

```csharp
Copy code
public class Order
{
    public int Id { get; private set; }
    public List<OrderLine> OrderLines { get; private set; }
    public decimal Total => OrderLines.Sum(line => line.Total);
}
```

Example IOrderRepository.cs:

```csharp
Copy code
public interface IOrderRepository
{
    void Add(Order order);
    Order GetById(int id);
}
```

Step 5: Implement the Application Layer

- Create use cases, such as placing an order.
- Implement commands and command handlers.
- Create DTOs for data transfer between layers.

Example PlaceOrderCommand.cs:

```csharp
Copy code
public class PlaceOrderCommand
{
```

CHAPTER 3: STRUCTURING YOUR SOLUTION FOR CLEAN ARCHITECTURE

```
    public List<OrderLineDto> OrderLines { get; set; }
}
```

Example PlaceOrderHandler.cs:

```csharp
Copy code
public class PlaceOrderHandler
{
    private readonly IOrderRepository _orderRepository;

    public PlaceOrderHandler(IOrderRepository orderRepository)
    {
        _orderRepository = orderRepository;
    }

    public void Handle(PlaceOrderCommand command)
    {
        var order = new Order { /* initialize with command data */ };
        _orderRepository.Add(order);
    }
}
```

Step 6: Implement the Infrastructure Layer

- Implement the SqlOrderRepository to interact with the SQL Server database.
- Use Entity Framework Core for data access.

Example SqlOrderRepository.cs:

```csharp
Copy code
public class SqlOrderRepository : IOrderRepository
{
    private readonly OrderContext _context;
```

```csharp
    public SqlOrderRepository(OrderContext context)
    {
        _context = context;
    }

    public void Add(Order order)
    {
        _context.Orders.Add(order);
        _context.SaveChanges();
    }

    public Order GetById(int id)
    {
        return _context.Orders.Include(o =>
        o.OrderLines).FirstOrDefault(o => o.Id == id);
    }
}
```

Step 7: Implement the UI Layer

- Create a simple API controller to handle HTTP requests related to orders.

Example OrderController.cs:

```
csharp
Copy code
[ApiController]
[Route("api/[controller]")]
public class OrderController : ControllerBase
{
    private readonly PlaceOrderHandler _placeOrderHandler;

    public OrderController(PlaceOrderHandler placeOrderHandler)
    {
        _placeOrderHandler = placeOrderHandler;
    }
```

CHAPTER 3: STRUCTURING YOUR SOLUTION FOR CLEAN ARCHITECTURE

```csharp
    [HttpPost]
    public IActionResult PlaceOrder
([FromBody] PlaceOrderCommand command)
    {
        _placeOrderHandler.Handle(command);
        return Ok();
    }
}
```

Step 8: Configure Dependency Injection in Startup

In your Startup.cs file, configure the DI container to register your services and repositories.

```csharp
Copy code
public void ConfigureServices
(IServiceCollection services)
{
    services.AddControllers();
    services.AddScoped<IOrderRepository, SqlOrderRepository>();
    services.AddScoped<PlaceOrderHandler>();
    services.AddDbContext<
OrderContext>(options => options.UseSqlServer(Configuration.
GetConnectionString
("DefaultConnection")));
}
```

Best Practices for Organizing a Clean Architecture Project

1. **Consistent Naming Conventions**: Adopt a consistent naming convention for classes, methods, and folders. This improves readability and maintainability.
2. **Keep the Project Modular**: If the application grows, consider splitting different modules into separate projects (e.g., a separate project for each feature set).
3. **Limit Dependencies**: Keep dependencies minimal. Only include those that are necessary for each layer.

4. **Document Your Architecture**: Maintain architectural documentation that explains the structure and design decisions. This is especially important for new team members or stakeholders.
5. **Regularly Review Code Structure**: As your application evolves, take the time to review the code structure and make adjustments as necessary.

Testing Your Clean Architecture Project

Testing is critical in ensuring the quality and reliability of your application. Clean Architecture facilitates easier testing due to its separation of concerns.

Unit Testing

- Use unit tests to validate the logic within each layer.
- Mock dependencies using frameworks like Moq to isolate tests.

Example of a unit test for PlaceOrderHandler:

```csharp
Copy code
[Fact]
public void Handle_ShouldAddOrderToRepository()
{
    // Arrange
    var mockRepository = new Mock<IOrderRepository>();
    var handler = new PlaceOrderHandler(mockRepository.Object);
    var command = new PlaceOrderCommand { /* initialize properties */ };

    // Act
    handler.Handle(command);

    // Assert
    mockRepository.Verify(r => r.Add(It.IsAny<Order>()), Times.Once);
}
```

Integration Testing

CHAPTER 3: STRUCTURING YOUR SOLUTION FOR CLEAN ARCHITECTURE

- Integration tests ensure that different components work together correctly.
- Test database interactions and the flow between layers.

Example of an integration test:

```csharp
Copy code
[Fact]
public void PlaceOrder_ShouldSaveToDatabase()
{
    // Arrange
    var options = new DbContextOptionsBuilder<OrderContext>()
.UseInMemoryDatabase("TestDatabase")
        .Options;

    using (var context = new OrderContext(options))
    {
        var repository = new SqlOrderRepository(context);
        var handler = new PlaceOrderHandler(repository);
        var command = new PlaceOrderCommand { /* initialize properties */ };

        // Act
        handler.Handle(command);

        // Assert
        var order = context.Orders.FirstOrDefault();
        Assert.NotNull(order);
        Assert.Equal(expectedValue, order.Property);
    }
}
```

Final Thoughts and Next Steps

In this chapter, you have learned how to structure your solution to implement Clean Architecture effectively. We covered the folder organization for each layer, the importance of separation of concerns, and how to implement the core components of a Clean Architecture application.

In the next chapter, we will delve into specific implementations of the Domain Layer, focusing on entities, value objects, aggregates, and domain services. We will also explore best practices for designing the Domain Layer to ensure your application remains maintainable and scalable.

Chapter 4: Implementing the Domain Layer

Introduction
- Overview of the Domain Layer's importance in Clean Architecture.
- Discussion on how the Domain Layer encapsulates business logic and rules, serving as the heart of the application.
- Explanation of the separation of concerns, emphasizing the need for a pure domain model that is independent of external systems.

Understanding the Role of the Domain Layer

The Domain Layer is the core of the application and contains the business logic that defines how the system behaves. Unlike the Application Layer, which coordinates tasks, or the Infrastructure Layer, which handles data storage and external interactions, the Domain Layer focuses on the entities, business rules, and operations that govern the system's functionality.

Key Responsibilities of the Domain Layer:

- **Business Logic**: Implements the rules that dictate how data can be created, stored, and manipulated.
- **State Management**: Manages the state of the business entities and ensures that invariants are maintained.

- **Encapsulation**: Hides implementation details from the rest of the application, exposing only necessary interfaces.

Entities

Entities are the core components of the Domain Layer. They represent distinct objects that have an identity and lifecycle. An entity is defined by its properties and behaviors, and its identity is what distinguishes it from other entities.

Defining Entities

- Entities must have a unique identifier, usually represented by a property called Id.
- They can contain various properties, methods, and behaviors that define their state and capabilities.

Example of an Entity: Order

```csharp
Copy code
public class Order
{
    public int Id { get; private set; }
    public DateTime OrderDate { get; private set; }
    public List<OrderLine> OrderLines { get; private set; } = new List<OrderLine>();

    public Order(DateTime orderDate)
    {
        OrderDate = orderDate;
    }

    public void AddOrderLine(OrderLine line)
    {
        OrderLines.Add(line);
    }
```

```csharp
    public decimal GetTotal()
    {
        return OrderLines.Sum(line => line.Total);
    }
}
```

In this example, the Order class defines an entity with an identity (Id), a creation date (OrderDate), and methods to add order lines and calculate totals.

Maintaining Invariants

Entities must enforce invariants to ensure the integrity of the data. Invariants are rules that must always hold true for an entity.

Example of Enforcing Invariants:

```csharp
Copy code
public class Order
{
    //...

    public void AddOrderLine(OrderLine line)
    {
        if (line.Quantity <= 0)
        {
            throw new InvalidOperationException("Quantity must be greater than zero.");
        }
        OrderLines.Add(line);
    }
}
```

Value Objects

Value Objects are another crucial concept in the Domain Layer. Unlike entities, value objects do not have a unique identity. Instead, they are defined solely by their attributes and represent descriptive aspects of the domain.

Characteristics of Value Objects:

- **Immutability**: Value objects should be immutable, meaning their state cannot change after creation.
- **Equality**: Equality is determined by the values of their properties, not by identity.

Example of a Value Object: Money

```csharp
Copy code
public class Money
{
    public decimal Amount { get; }
    public string Currency { get; }

    public Money(decimal amount, string currency)
    {
        if (amount < 0) throw new
        ArgumentOutOfRangeException(nameof(amount), "Amount must
        be positive.");
        Amount = amount;
        Currency = currency;
    }

    public static Money operator +(Money a, Money b)
    {
        if (a.Currency != b.Currency)
            throw new InvalidOperationException("Cannot add
            different currencies.");
        return new Money(a.Amount + b.Amount, a.Currency);
    }
}
```

In this example, the Money class represents a value object with properties for Amount and Currency. It is immutable and includes an operator for adding two Money objects together, enforcing a business rule that both amounts must have the same currency.

Aggregates

Aggregates are a grouping of related entities and value objects treated as a single unit for data changes. Each aggregate has a root entity (the aggregate root), which is the only member of the aggregate that external components can reference.

Defining Aggregates

- Aggregates help maintain consistency by ensuring that all operations on the aggregate root also affect related entities.
- Use aggregates to enforce business rules that span multiple entities.

Example of an Aggregate: Order and OrderLine

```csharp
Copy code
public class Order
{
    public int Id { get; private set; }
    public List<OrderLine> OrderLines { get; private set; } = new List<OrderLine>();

    public void AddOrderLine(Product product, int quantity)
    {
        var orderLine = new OrderLine(product, quantity);
        OrderLines.Add(orderLine);
    }
}
```

In this example, Order acts as the aggregate root that manages a collection of OrderLine entities. The AddOrderLine method ensures that new order lines are created in the context of the order, maintaining aggregate integrity.

Domain Services

Domain Services are used to encapsulate domain logic that does not naturally fit within a single entity or value object. They provide an alternative way to perform operations that require collaboration between multiple entities or involve complex business rules.

Characteristics of Domain Services:

- **Stateless**: Domain services typically do not hold state; they perform actions based on inputs and return results.
- **Encapsulate Business Logic**: They encapsulate business logic that spans multiple entities or value objects.

Example of a Domain Service: Order Processing Service

```csharp
Copy code
public class OrderProcessingService
{
    private readonly IOrderRepository _orderRepository;

    public OrderProcessingService(IOrderRepository orderRepository)
    {
        _orderRepository = orderRepository;
    }

    public void ProcessOrder(Order order)
    {
        // Business logic for processing the order
        order.CalculateTotal();
        _orderRepository.Add(order);
    }
}
```

In this example, the OrderProcessingService takes an order and processes it, encapsulating the logic for calculating totals and persisting the order.

Implementing the Domain Layer: Best Practices

When implementing the Domain Layer, adhering to best practices ensures a robust, maintainable codebase.

1. **Keep the Domain Layer Pure**: Avoid dependencies on external systems (like databases or APIs) in the Domain Layer. This allows for isolated testing and maintenance.
2. **Use Interfaces**: Define interfaces for repositories and services to promote loose coupling. Implementations of these interfaces should

reside in the Infrastructure Layer.
3. **Encapsulate Business Logic**: Keep business logic within entities, value objects, and domain services. This encapsulation makes the logic reusable and easier to maintain.
4. **Define Invariants**: Ensure that your entities enforce business rules and maintain data integrity. Throw exceptions for invalid states to prevent unwanted behavior.
5. **Adopt a Rich Domain Model**: Favor a rich domain model that encapsulates behavior rather than a data-centric model. This means that entities should contain methods that operate on their state, rather than exposing data for manipulation elsewhere.
6. **Test the Domain Layer**: Write unit tests for entities, value objects, and domain services to ensure they behave as expected. Mock dependencies where necessary to isolate tests.

Using Domain Events

Domain events are a powerful mechanism for managing side effects within your domain model. They represent something that has happened in the domain and can trigger actions in other parts of the system.

Implementing Domain Events

- Define domain events as simple classes or records that carry data related to the event.

Example of a Domain Event: OrderPlacedEvent

```csharp
Copy code
public class OrderPlacedEvent
{
    public Order Order { get; }

    public OrderPlacedEvent(Order order)
    {
```

```csharp
        Order = order;
    }
}
```

- Publish events from within your domain model after state changes occur.

Publishing Events from the Domain Layer:

```csharp
Copy code
public class Order
{
    //...

    public void PlaceOrder()
    {
        // Logic for placing an order
        DomainEvents.Raise(new OrderPlacedEvent(this));
    }
}
```

Handling Domain Events

- Implement a mechanism for handling domain events, usually within the Application Layer or Infrastructure Layer.
- Use an event bus or a simple mediator pattern to manage event subscriptions and handlers.

Example of Handling Domain Events:

```csharp
Copy code
public class OrderPlacedEventHandler :
IEventHandler<OrderPlacedEvent>
```

```csharp
{
    public void Handle(OrderPlacedEvent domainEvent)
    {
        // Logic for handling the event (e.g., send notification)
    }
}
```

Example Use Case: Building an Order Management System

Let's bring together the concepts discussed so far by implementing an Order Management System using the Domain Layer principles outlined.

1. Define the Domain Model

Begin by defining your core entities and value objects.

Entities:

```csharp
Copy code
public class Order
{
    public int Id { get; private set; }
    public List<OrderLine> OrderLines { get; private set; } = new List<OrderLine>();
    public decimal Total => OrderLines.Sum(line => line.Total);

    public void AddOrderLine(Product product, int quantity)
    {
        var line = new OrderLine(product, quantity);
        OrderLines.Add(line);
        DomainEvents.Raise(new OrderLineAddedEvent(this, line));
    }
}

public class OrderLine
{
    public Product Product { get; }
    public int Quantity { get; }
    public decimal Total => Product.Price * Quantity;

    public OrderLine(Product product, int quantity)
```

```csharp
    {
        Product = product;
        Quantity = quantity;
    }
}
```

Value Objects:

```csharp
Copy code
public class Product
{
    public int Id { get; }
    public string Name { get; }
    public decimal Price { get; }

    public Product(int id, string name, decimal price)
    {
        Id = id;
        Name = name;
        Price = price;
    }
}
```

2. Implement Domain Services

Create domain services to handle complex business operations.

Order Processing Service:

```csharp
Copy code
public class OrderProcessingService
{
    private readonly IOrderRepository _orderRepository;

    public OrderProcessingService(IOrderRepository orderRepository)
    {
        _orderRepository = orderRepository;
```

CHAPTER 4: IMPLEMENTING THE DOMAIN LAYER

```csharp
    }

    public void ProcessOrder(Order order)
    {
        // Process order
        order.PlaceOrder();
        _orderRepository.Add(order);
    }
}
```

3. Define Domain Events

Define events to manage side effects and notify other parts of the system.

OrderLineAddedEvent:

```csharp
Copy code
public class OrderLineAddedEvent
{
    public Order Order { get; }
    public OrderLine OrderLine { get; }

    public OrderLineAddedEvent(Order order, OrderLine orderLine)
    {
        Order = order;
        OrderLine = orderLine;
    }
}
```

4. Testing the Domain Layer

Unit tests are essential to ensure the correctness of your domain logic.

Testing Order Creation:

```csharp
Copy code
[Fact]
public void AddingOrderLine_ShouldIncreaseTotal()
{
```

```
    // Arrange
    var order = new Order();
    var product = new Product(1, "Test Product", 10.00m);

    // Act
    order.AddOrderLine(product, 2);

    // Assert
    Assert.Equal(20.00m, order.Total);
}
```

Conclusion

The Domain Layer is a critical component of Clean Architecture, serving as the foundation for business logic and encapsulating the rules that govern how the system operates. By effectively implementing entities, value objects, aggregates, and domain services, developers can create a robust and maintainable codebase.

This chapter has outlined the key concepts and best practices for implementing the Domain Layer. In the next chapter, we will explore the Application Layer, where we will focus on orchestrating use cases, handling commands and queries, and implementing business workflows.

By following the principles laid out in this chapter, you will ensure that your Domain Layer remains clean, maintainable, and adaptable to changing business requirements.

Chapter 5: Building the Application Layer

Introduction
- Overview of the Application Layer's purpose in Clean Architecture.
- Explanation of how the Application Layer serves as a bridge between the Domain Layer and external systems (like the UI and Infrastructure).
- Discussion of the importance of orchestrating use cases and managing the flow of data within the application.

Understanding the Application Layer

The Application Layer is where the actual use cases of the application are defined and implemented. Unlike the Domain Layer, which focuses on business rules and logic, the Application Layer coordinates tasks and manages the interactions between various components, such as the Domain Layer, Infrastructure Layer, and UI.

Key Responsibilities of the Application Layer:

1. **Orchestrating Use Cases**: The Application Layer encapsulates the use cases that the system must perform, such as creating an order, processing payments, or retrieving customer details.
2. **Handling Commands and Queries**: It distinguishes between commands (which change the state of the system) and queries (which retrieve data).

3. **Interacting with Repositories**: The Application Layer uses repositories to perform operations on domain entities and value objects.
4. **Managing Transactions**: It ensures that operations that need to be executed together are done within a transaction, maintaining data consistency.
5. **Handling External Services**: The Application Layer can interact with external systems, such as APIs, to complete its tasks.

Defining Use Cases

Use cases define the actions that the system can perform and encapsulate the specific business logic required for each action. Each use case should represent a single responsibility and be focused on a specific task or business requirement.

Creating a Use Case

1. **Identify the Use Case**: Determine what specific action the system should perform based on business requirements.
2. **Define Inputs and Outputs**: Specify what data will be needed to execute the use case and what the expected results will be.
3. **Implement the Use Case**: Create a command or query object that represents the action, along with a corresponding handler to perform the logic.

Example: Place Order Use Case

1. **Identify the Use Case**: "Place an Order."
2. **Define Inputs**: Order details, such as customer information and ordered items.
3. **Define Outputs**: Confirmation of the order, including order ID and status.

PlaceOrderCommand.cs

CHAPTER 5: BUILDING THE APPLICATION LAYER

```csharp
Copy code
public class PlaceOrderCommand
{
    public int CustomerId { get; set; }
    public List<OrderLineDto> OrderLines { get; set; }
}
```

PlaceOrderHandler.cs

```csharp
Copy code
public class PlaceOrderHandler
{
    private readonly IOrderRepository _orderRepository;

    public PlaceOrderHandler(IOrderRepository orderRepository)
    {
        _orderRepository = orderRepository;
    }

    public void Handle(PlaceOrderCommand command)
    {
        var order = new Order(DateTime.UtcNow);
        foreach (var line in command.OrderLines)
        {
            var product = new Product(line.ProductId,
            line.Quantity); // Assuming Product is already fetched.
            order.AddOrderLine(product, line.Quantity);
        }
        _orderRepository.Add(order);
    }
}
```

Command and Query Handlers

In Clean Architecture, commands and queries are treated distinctly to maintain clear separation of concerns. Commands are used for actions that change the state of the application, while queries are used to retrieve data without modifying it.

1. Command Handlers

Command handlers are responsible for processing commands. They receive commands, validate inputs, interact with the Domain Layer, and manage the persistence of changes.

Example: Command Handler for Updating an Order

```csharp
Copy code
public class UpdateOrderHandler
{
    private readonly IOrderRepository _orderRepository;

    public UpdateOrderHandler(IOrderRepository orderRepository)
    {
        _orderRepository = orderRepository;
    }

    public void Handle(UpdateOrderCommand command)
    {
        var order = _orderRepository.GetById(command.OrderId);
        if (order == null)
        {
            throw new NotFoundException("Order not found.");
        }
        // Update order logic
        order.UpdateDetails(command.NewDetails);
        _orderRepository.Update(order);
    }
}
```

2. Query Handlers

Query handlers are responsible for retrieving data. They process queries and return the requested information, often in the form of DTOs.

Example: Query Handler for Getting Order Details

```csharp
Copy code
```

CHAPTER 5: BUILDING THE APPLICATION LAYER

```
public class GetOrderDetailsQueryHandler
{
    private readonly IOrderRepository _orderRepository;

    public GetOrderDetailsQueryHandler(IOrderRepository
    orderRepository)
    {
        _orderRepository = orderRepository;
    }

    public OrderDetailsDto Handle(GetOrderDetailsQuery query)
    {
        var order = _orderRepository.GetById(query.OrderId);
        if (order == null)
        {
            throw new NotFoundException("Order not found.");
        }
        return new OrderDetailsDto
        {
            Id = order.Id,
            Total = order.Total,
            OrderDate = order.OrderDate,
            // Map additional properties as needed
        };
    }
}
```

Application Services

Application services provide an interface for the use cases of the application. They encapsulate the command and query handlers and serve as a central point for coordinating interactions between different components.

Creating an Application Service

1. **Define the Application Service Interface**: Specify the methods that the application service will expose.
2. **Implement the Application Service**: Use dependency injection to access command and query handlers, coordinating the flow of data.

Example: OrderService

```csharp
public interface IOrderService
{
    void PlaceOrder(PlaceOrderCommand command);
    OrderDetailsDto GetOrderDetails(int orderId);
}

public class OrderService : IOrderService
{
    private readonly PlaceOrderHandler _placeOrderHandler;
    private readonly GetOrderDetailsQueryHandler
    _getOrderDetailsHandler;

    public OrderService(PlaceOrderHandler placeOrderHandler,
    GetOrderDetailsQueryHandler getOrderDetailsHandler)
    {
        _placeOrderHandler = placeOrderHandler;
        _getOrderDetailsHandler = getOrderDetailsHandler;
    }

    public void PlaceOrder(PlaceOrderCommand command)
    {
        _placeOrderHandler.Handle(command);
    }

    public OrderDetailsDto GetOrderDetails(int orderId)
    {
        var query = new GetOrderDetailsQuery { OrderId = orderId };
        return _getOrderDetailsHandler.Handle(query);
    }
}
```

Managing Transactions

In the Application Layer, it's important to manage transactions effectively to ensure data consistency. When performing operations that involve multiple steps (e.g., placing an order and updating inventory), you may need to ensure that all operations succeed or fail together.

Using Unit of Work Pattern

The Unit of Work pattern can help manage transactions across multiple repositories. It tracks changes and ensures that all updates are committed or rolled back together.

Example of a Unit of Work Implementation

```csharp
Copy code
public interface IUnitOfWork
{
    void Commit();
    void Rollback();
}

public class UnitOfWork : IUnitOfWork
{
    private readonly OrderContext _context;

    public UnitOfWork(OrderContext context)
    {
        _context = context;
    }

    public void Commit()
    {
        _context.SaveChanges();
    }

    public void Rollback()
    {
        // Rollback logic if using a transaction
    }
}
```

Integrating Unit of Work with Application Services

Integrate the Unit of Work within your application services to ensure all operations are performed within a transaction.

Example: Modifying the OrderService to Use Unit of Work

```csharp
public class OrderService : IOrderService
{
    private readonly PlaceOrderHandler _placeOrderHandler;
    private readonly GetOrderDetailsQueryHandler
    _getOrderDetailsHandler;
    private readonly IUnitOfWork _unitOfWork;

    public OrderService(PlaceOrderHandler placeOrderHandler,
    GetOrderDetailsQueryHandler getOrderDetailsHandler,
    IUnitOfWork unitOfWork)
    {
        _placeOrderHandler = placeOrderHandler;
        _getOrderDetailsHandler = getOrderDetailsHandler;
        _unitOfWork = unitOfWork;
    }

    public void PlaceOrder(PlaceOrderCommand command)
    {
        try
        {
            _placeOrderHandler.Handle(command);
            _unitOfWork.Commit();
        }
        catch (Exception)
        {
            _unitOfWork.Rollback();
            throw; // or handle exception
        }
    }

    public OrderDetailsDto GetOrderDetails(int orderId)
    {
        var query = new GetOrderDetailsQuery { OrderId = orderId };
        return _getOrderDetailsHandler.Handle(query);
    }
}
```

CHAPTER 5: BUILDING THE APPLICATION LAYER

Handling External Services

The Application Layer often interacts with external services, such as payment processors, email services, or messaging queues. Abstracting these interactions behind interfaces promotes loose coupling and makes testing easier.

Example of Integrating a Payment Service

1. **Define an Interface**: Create an interface for the payment gateway.
2. **Implement the Service**: Provide a concrete implementation that handles the API interactions.

Example: Payment Gateway Interface

```csharp
Copy code
public interface IPaymentGateway
{
    void Charge(Money amount);
}
```

Example: Stripe Payment Gateway Implementation

```csharp
Copy code
public class StripePaymentGateway : IPaymentGateway
{
    public void Charge(Money amount)
    {
        // Call to Stripe API to charge the amount
    }
}
```

Using the Payment Gateway in the Application Layer

Integrate the payment gateway within the use cases or application services.

Example: Integrating Payment in the PlaceOrderHandler

```csharp
Copy code
public class PlaceOrderHandler
{
    private readonly IOrderRepository _orderRepository;
    private readonly IPaymentGateway _paymentGateway;

    public PlaceOrderHandler(IOrderRepository orderRepository, 
    IPaymentGateway paymentGateway)
    {
        _orderRepository = orderRepository;
        _paymentGateway = paymentGateway;
    }

    public void Handle(PlaceOrderCommand command)
    {
        var order = new Order(DateTime.UtcNow);
        foreach (var line in command.OrderLines)
        {
            var product = new Product(line.ProductId, 
            line.Quantity); // Assuming Product is already fetched.
            order.AddOrderLine(product, line.Quantity);
        }

        // Charge payment
        var totalAmount = new Money(order.Total, "USD"); // 
        Example currency
        _paymentGateway.Charge(totalAmount);

        _orderRepository.Add(order);
    }
}
```

Implementing Validation in the Application Layer

Validation is a crucial aspect of the Application Layer, ensuring that the data being processed meets the required criteria. It can involve checking input data for required fields, format, and business logic rules.

Using FluentValidation for Input Validation

FluentValidation is a popular library for implementing validation in .NET applications. It allows you to define validation rules for your DTOs in a clean and expressive manner.

Example: Defining Validation Rules for PlaceOrderCommand

```csharp
Copy code
public class PlaceOrderCommandValidator : AbstractValidator<PlaceOrderCommand>
{
    public PlaceOrderCommandValidator()
    {
        RuleFor(x => x.CustomerId).GreaterThan(0).WithMessage("Customer ID must be greater than zero.");
        RuleFor(x => x.OrderLines).NotEmpty().WithMessage("Order must have at least one order line.");
    }
}
```

Integrating Validation into the Application Service

Ensure validation is performed before executing commands within your application service.

Example: Validating PlaceOrderCommand in OrderService

```csharp
Copy code
public class OrderService : IOrderService
{
    private readonly PlaceOrderHandler _placeOrderHandler;
    private readonly IValidator<PlaceOrderCommand> _validator;

    public OrderService(PlaceOrderHandler placeOrderHandler, IValidator<PlaceOrderCommand> validator)
    {
        _placeOrderHandler = placeOrderHandler;
        _validator = validator;
    }
```

```csharp
public void PlaceOrder(PlaceOrderCommand command)
{
    var validationResult = _validator.Validate(command);
    if (!validationResult.IsValid)
    {
        throw new ValidationException(validationResult.Errors);
    }

    _placeOrderHandler.Handle(command);
}
```

Testing the Application Layer

Testing is crucial to ensure that the Application Layer behaves as expected. The focus should be on unit tests for command handlers, query handlers, and application services.

Unit Testing Command Handlers

Unit tests for command handlers verify that the logic is executed correctly and that the state changes are as expected.

Example: Unit Test for PlaceOrderHandler

```csharp
Copy code
[Fact]
public void Handle_ShouldAddOrder()
{
    // Arrange
    var mockRepository = new Mock<IOrderRepository>();
    var handler = new PlaceOrderHandler(mockRepository.Object);
    var command = new PlaceOrderCommand { /* initialize properties */ };

    // Act
    handler.Handle(command);

    // Assert
    mockRepository.Verify(r => r.Add(It.IsAny<Order>()),
```

```
    Times.Once);
}
```

Unit Testing Query Handlers

Similarly, unit tests for query handlers ensure that the retrieval logic is accurate.

Example: Unit Test for GetOrderDetailsQueryHandler

```csharp
Copy code
[Fact]
public void Handle_ShouldReturnOrderDetails()
{
    // Arrange
    var mockRepository = new Mock<IOrderRepository>();
    var handler = new
GetOrderDetailsQueryHandler(mockRepository.Object);
    var query = new GetOrderDetailsQuery { OrderId = 1 };
    mockRepository.Setup(r =>
r.GetById(query.OrderId)).Returns(new Order(/* initialize
order */));

    // Act
    var result = handler.Handle(query);

    // Assert
    Assert.NotNull(result);
    Assert.Equal(1, result.Id);
}
```

Best Practices for the Application Layer

1. **Keep Use Cases Focused**: Each use case should encapsulate a single business operation. This simplifies the logic and makes it easier to understand.
2. **Use Interfaces**: Define interfaces for command and query handlers to promote loose coupling and facilitate testing.

3. **Implement Validation**: Use validation libraries like FluentValidation to enforce business rules before processing commands.
4. **Isolate External Dependencies**: Abstract external services behind interfaces, making it easier to swap out implementations or mock them during testing.
5. **Use Unit of Work**: When multiple repositories are involved, utilize the Unit of Work pattern to manage transactions effectively.
6. **Test Extensively**: Write unit tests for all handlers and application services to ensure they function correctly and maintain their intended behaviors.

Conclusion

The Application Layer plays a critical role in Clean Architecture, orchestrating the various use cases of the application while maintaining clear boundaries with the Domain Layer and Infrastructure Layer. By effectively defining commands and queries, managing data flow, and integrating external services, developers can create a robust and maintainable codebase.

In this chapter, we explored the key concepts and responsibilities of the Application Layer, as well as best practices for implementing and testing it. With a solid foundation in place, the next chapter will delve into the Infrastructure Layer, focusing on data access, repository patterns, and interactions with external systems.

Chapter 6: Implementing the Infrastructure Layer

Introduction
- Overview of the Infrastructure Layer and its role in Clean Architecture.
- Explanation of how the Infrastructure Layer interacts with external systems (databases, APIs, etc.).
- Discussion of the importance of decoupling the infrastructure from the business logic to maintain a clean architecture.

Understanding the Infrastructure Layer

The Infrastructure Layer serves as the bridge between the application and external systems. It is responsible for implementing data access, interacting with external services, and handling cross-cutting concerns such as logging and configuration management.

Key Responsibilities of the Infrastructure Layer:

1. **Data Persistence**: Managing interactions with databases, including creating, reading, updating, and deleting data.
2. **External Service Integration**: Interfacing with third-party services such as payment gateways, email providers, and messaging systems.

3. **Logging and Monitoring**: Capturing application events and errors for diagnostic purposes.
4. **Configuration Management**: Managing application settings and configurations, often sourced from appsettings.json or environment variables.

Implementing Data Access in the Infrastructure Layer

Data access in the Infrastructure Layer can be achieved using various patterns, with the **Repository Pattern** being one of the most common approaches. The Repository Pattern abstracts the data layer, allowing the application to work with a simplified API while hiding the complexities of data storage and retrieval.

1. The Repository Pattern

The Repository Pattern provides a way to encapsulate data access logic, making it easier to manage and test.

Benefits of the Repository Pattern:

- **Abstraction**: Abstracts the data access logic from the application logic, promoting separation of concerns.
- **Testability**: Allows for easier unit testing by enabling the use of mocks or in-memory repositories.
- **Flexibility**: Makes it easier to switch out data access strategies or technologies without affecting the application code.

2. Defining Repository Interfaces

In the Infrastructure Layer, you should define interfaces for your repositories. These interfaces will specify the methods for data access, ensuring that the implementation can vary without impacting the rest of the application.

Example: IOrderRepository

```
csharp
Copy code
```

```csharp
public interface IOrderRepository
{
    void Add(Order order);
    Order GetById(int id);
    IEnumerable<Order> GetAll();
}
```

3. Implementing the Repository

Once you have defined the repository interface, the next step is to implement it. This is where you connect to the actual data source (e.g., a SQL database).

Example: SqlOrderRepository Implementation

```csharp
Copy code
public class SqlOrderRepository : IOrderRepository
{
    private readonly OrderContext _context;

    public SqlOrderRepository(OrderContext context)
    {
        _context = context;
    }

    public void Add(Order order)
    {
        _context.Orders.Add(order);
        _context.SaveChanges();
    }

    public Order GetById(int id)
    {
        return _context.Orders.Include(o =>
        o.OrderLines).FirstOrDefault(o => o.Id == id);
    }

    public IEnumerable<Order> GetAll()
    {
```

```
        return _context.Orders.Include(o =>
o.OrderLines).ToList();
    }
}
```

4. Using Entity Framework Core

Entity Framework Core (EF Core) is a popular Object-Relational Mapping (ORM) framework that simplifies data access in .NET applications. It allows you to work with databases using strongly typed objects, removing the need for complex SQL queries in many scenarios.

Setting Up EF Core

1. **Install NuGet Packages**: Make sure you have the necessary EF Core packages installed.
2. **Configure DbContext**: Create a DbContext class that represents the database context.

Example: OrderContext

```csharp
Copy code
public class OrderContext : DbContext
{
    public DbSet<Order> Orders { get; set; }

    public OrderContext(DbContextOptions<OrderContext> options)
        : base(options) { }

    protected override void OnModelCreating(ModelBuilder modelBuilder)
    {
        modelBuilder.Entity<Order>()
            .ToTable("Orders");
```

```
        modelBuilder.Entity<OrderLine>()
            .ToTable("OrderLines");
    }
}
```

Configuring the Database Connection

In your appsettings.json, configure the connection string for your database.

```json
Copy code
{
    "ConnectionStrings": {
        "DefaultConnection":
        "Server=your_server;Database=OrderDB;User
        Id=your_user;Password=your_password;"
    }
}
```

In the Startup.cs, configure EF Core to use SQL Server:

```csharp
Copy code
public void ConfigureServices
(IServiceCollection services)
{
    services.AddDbContext<OrderContext>(options =>
        options.UseSqlServer(Configuration.
GetConnectionString("DefaultConnection")));

    services.AddScoped<IOrderRepository,
SqlOrderRepository>();
}
```

Implementing External Service Integration

The Infrastructure Layer also handles interactions with external services, such as payment gateways or email services. This can be achieved by defining interfaces for these services and implementing them within the Infrastructure

Layer.

1. Defining External Service Interfaces

Similar to repositories, external services should be defined with interfaces. This allows you to swap implementations or mock them for testing.

Example: IPaymentGateway

```csharp
Copy code
public interface IPaymentGateway
{
    void Charge(Money amount);
}
```

2. Implementing External Services

Create concrete implementations for these services, encapsulating the logic for calling the external APIs.

Example: StripePaymentGateway Implementation

```csharp
Copy code
public class StripePaymentGateway : IPaymentGateway
{
    public void Charge(Money amount)
    {
        // Logic to integrate with the Stripe API to charge the amount
        // This might involve creating a payment intent, handling
        responses, etc.
    }
}
```

3. Using Dependency Injection for External Services

Register the external service implementations in the DI container within Startup.cs.

```csharp
Copy code
public void ConfigureServices
(IServiceCollection services)
{
    services.AddScoped<IPaymentGateway,
StripePaymentGateway>();
}
```

Handling Cross-Cutting Concerns

Cross-cutting concerns, such as logging, caching, and error handling, are typically managed in the Infrastructure Layer. It's essential to address these concerns to maintain a clean architecture while ensuring that the core logic remains focused on business rules.

1. Implementing Logging

Using a logging library, such as Serilog or NLog, can help capture logs throughout your application.

Example: Setting Up Logging with Serilog

1. Install the Serilog NuGet package.
2. Configure Serilog in the Program.cs.

```csharp
Copy code
public class Program
{
    public static void Main(string[] args)
    {
        Log.Logger = new LoggerConfiguration()
            .WriteTo.Console()
            .CreateLogger();

        CreateHostBuilder(args).Build().Run();
    }
```

```
    public static IHostBuilder
CreateHostBuilder(string[] args) =>
        Host.CreateDefaultBuilder(args)
            .UseSerilog() // Use Serilog for logging
            .ConfigureWebHostDefaults(webBuilder =>
            {
                webBuilder.UseStartup<Startup>();
            });
}
```

2. Managing Caching

Caching can improve performance by storing frequently accessed data in memory.

Example: Using MemoryCache

1. Install the Microsoft.Extensions.Caching.Memory NuGet package.
2. Register IMemoryCache in the DI container.

```
csharp
Copy code
public void ConfigureServices
(IServiceCollection services)
{
    services.AddMemoryCache();
}
```

1. Use IMemoryCache in your services.

```
csharp
Copy code
public class CachedOrderRepository
 : IOrderRepository
```

CHAPTER 6: IMPLEMENTING THE INFRASTRUCTURE LAYER

```csharp
{
    private readonly IMemoryCache _cache;
    private readonly IOrderRepository _repository;

    public CachedOrderRepository
(IMemoryCache cache, IOrderRepository repository)
    {
        _cache = cache;
        _repository = repository;
    }

    public Order GetById(int id)
    {
        if (!_cache.TryGetValue
($"Order-{id}", out Order order))
        {
            order = _repository.GetById(id);
      _cache.Set($"Order-{id}", order);
        }
        return order;
    }
}
```

3. Error Handling and Exception Management

Implementing a centralized error-handling mechanism can help manage exceptions consistently across your application.

Example: Global Error Handling Middleware

```csharp
Copy code
public class ErrorHandlingMiddleware
{
    private readonly RequestDelegate _next;

    public ErrorHandlingMiddleware
(RequestDelegate next)
    {
        _next = next;
```

```
    }

    public async Task InvokeAsync
(HttpContext context)
    {
        try
        {
            await _next(context);
        }
        catch (Exception ex)
        {
            // Log the error and return a generic error response
            Log.Error(ex,
"An unhandled exception occurred.");
            context.Response.StatusCode =
            (int)HttpStatusCode.InternalServerError;
await context.Response.
WriteAsync("An error occurred
while processing your request.");
        }
    }
}
```

Registering the Middleware in Startup

```
csharp
Copy code
public void Configure(IApplicationBuilder app, IWebHostEnvironment env)
{
    app.UseMiddleware<ErrorHandlingMiddleware>();
    // Other middleware registrations
}
```

Testing the Infrastructure Layer

Testing is critical for ensuring the reliability of the Infrastructure Layer. This involves testing repositories, external service integrations, and middleware.

CHAPTER 6: IMPLEMENTING THE INFRASTRUCTURE LAYER

1. Unit Testing Repositories

Unit tests for repositories validate that data access logic works correctly.

Example: Unit Test for SqlOrderRepository

```csharp
Copy code
[Fact]
public void GetById_ShouldReturnCorrectOrder()
{
    // Arrange
    var options = new DbContextOptionsBuilder<OrderContext>()
        .UseInMemoryDatabase("TestDatabase")
        .Options;

    using (var context = new OrderContext(options))
    {
        var order = new Order(/* parameters */);
        context.Orders.Add(order);
        context.SaveChanges();
    }

    using (var context = new OrderContext(options))
    {
        var repository = new SqlOrderRepository(context);

        // Act
        var result = repository.GetById(order.Id);

        // Assert
        Assert.NotNull(result);
        Assert.Equal(order.Id, result.Id);
    }
}
```

2. Integration Testing External Services

Integration tests ensure that the Infrastructure Layer interacts correctly with external services.

Example: Integration Test for StripePaymentGateway

```csharp
Copy code
[Fact]
public void Charge_ShouldSendPaymentToStripe()
{
    // Arrange
    var paymentGateway = new StripePaymentGateway();

    // Act
    paymentGateway.Charge(new Money(100, "USD"));

    // Assert: Check Stripe account
for the transaction or mock the call to verify behavior.
}
```

3. Testing Middleware

Unit tests can also be written for middleware to ensure that it handles errors correctly.

Example: Unit Test for ErrorHandlingMiddleware

```csharp
Copy code
[Fact]
public async Task InvokeAsync_ShouldHandleException()
{
    // Arrange
    var context = new DefaultHttpContext();
    var middleware =
new ErrorHandlingMiddleware
(async (innerHttpContext) =>
    {
        throw new Exception("Test exception");
    });

    // Act
```

```
    await middleware.InvokeAsync(context);

    // Assert
    Assert.Equal((int)HttpStatusCode.
InternalServerError, context.
Response.StatusCode);
}
```

Best Practices for the Infrastructure Layer

1. **Keep Infrastructure Concerns Separate**: Ensure that the Infrastructure Layer is focused on data access and external integrations without intertwining with business logic.
2. **Use Interfaces for Data Access**: Define interfaces for repositories and services to promote loose coupling and enable easier testing and implementation swapping.
3. **Implement Unit of Work**: Use the Unit of Work pattern to manage transactions that span multiple repositories, ensuring data consistency.
4. **Implement Proper Logging**: Integrate logging across the Infrastructure Layer to capture important events and errors for later analysis.
5. **Manage Configuration Effectively**: Use configuration management techniques to centralize application settings and environment-specific configurations.
6. **Focus on Testing**: Write extensive unit and integration tests for the Infrastructure Layer to ensure that data access and external integrations work as expected.

Conclusion

The Infrastructure Layer is a vital component of Clean Architecture, responsible for data persistence, external service integration, and handling cross-cutting concerns. By implementing effective data access patterns, leveraging external services, and following best practices, developers can create a robust and maintainable infrastructure that supports the application.

In this chapter, we have explored the key concepts of the Infrastructure

Layer, including repository implementations, external service integrations, and best practices for managing cross-cutting concerns. In the next chapter, we will discuss the User Interface Layer, focusing on how to effectively present data and interact with users while adhering to Clean Architecture principles.

Chapter 7: Building the User Interface Layer

Introduction
- Overview of the User Interface (UI) Layer's role in Clean Architecture.
- Explanation of how the UI Layer interacts with the Application Layer and presents data to the user.
- Importance of maintaining separation of concerns and ensuring a clean, responsive user experience.

Understanding the User Interface Layer

The User Interface Layer is the entry point of the application, responsible for presenting information to users and capturing user input. This layer can encompass various UI technologies and patterns, including web applications, mobile apps, desktop applications, and APIs.

Key Responsibilities of the UI Layer:

1. **Presentation of Data**: Displaying data retrieved from the Application Layer in a user-friendly manner.
2. **User Interaction**: Capturing user input and translating it into commands for the Application Layer.

3. **Routing**: Managing navigation and state within the application.
4. **User Experience (UX)**: Ensuring that the application is intuitive and accessible for users.

Designing the User Interface Layer

The design of the UI Layer is crucial for providing a good user experience. Here are key concepts and patterns to consider:

1. UI Patterns

Understanding common UI patterns can help structure the UI Layer effectively. Some popular patterns include:

- **Model-View-Controller (MVC)**: Separates the application into three interconnected components. The Model represents the data, the View displays the data, and the Controller handles input and updates the Model.
- **Model-View-ViewModel (MVVM)**: Primarily used in XAML-based applications (like WPF or Xamarin), this pattern separates the UI logic from the business logic. The ViewModel exposes data and commands to the View, which binds to them.
- **Component-Based Architecture**: Popular in frameworks like React and Angular, this pattern promotes building reusable UI components that encapsulate their behavior and state.

2. Choosing the Right UI Technology

Depending on the application requirements and target platforms, various UI technologies can be employed:

- **ASP.NET Core MVC**: Ideal for building server-rendered web applications with a rich UI.
- **ASP.NET Core Web API**: Suitable for building APIs that serve data to client applications (web, mobile, etc.).
- **Blazor**: A framework for building interactive web applications using C# instead of JavaScript.
- **Xamarin**: Used for building cross-platform mobile applications with a

CHAPTER 7: BUILDING THE USER INTERFACE LAYER

shared codebase in C#.

Implementing the User Interface Layer with ASP.NET Core MVC

For the purpose of this chapter, we will focus on building a web application using ASP.NET Core MVC. This framework provides a robust foundation for developing server-side rendered applications while adhering to the principles of Clean Architecture.

1. Setting Up an ASP.NET Core MVC Project

To create an ASP.NET Core MVC application, follow these steps:

1. **Create a New Project**:

- Open Visual Studio and select **Create a new project**.
- Choose **ASP.NET Core Web Application**.
- Name your project (e.g., OrderManagementUI) and select the location.
- Choose the **Web Application (Model-View-Controller)** template.

1. **Install Necessary NuGet Packages**:

- Open the NuGet Package Manager Console and run:

```bash
Copy code
Install-Package Microsoft.AspNetCore.Mvc
Install-Package Microsoft.AspNetCore.Mvc.ViewFeatures
```

1. **Configure the Project**:

- Set up the MVC services in Startup.cs.

```csharp
Copy code
public void ConfigureServices(IServiceCollection services)
{
    services.AddControllersWithViews();
    services.AddScoped<IOrderService, OrderService>(); // Register application services
}
```

2. Creating Controllers

Controllers handle incoming HTTP requests, orchestrating the flow of data between the UI and the application layer.

Example: OrderController

```csharp
Copy code
public class OrderController : Controller
{
    private readonly IOrderService _orderService;

    public OrderController(IOrderService orderService)
    {
        _orderService = orderService;
    }

    [HttpGet]
    public IActionResult Index()
    {
        var orders = _orderService.GetAllOrders(); // Fetch orders from the service
        return View(orders);
// Return the view with the order list
    }

    [HttpPost]
    public IActionResult Create(PlaceOrderCommand command)
    {
```

CHAPTER 7: BUILDING THE USER INTERFACE LAYER

```
        if (!ModelState.IsValid)
        {
            return View(command);
// Return to the view with validation errors
        }

        _orderService.PlaceOrder(command);
        return RedirectToAction("Index");
// Redirect to the order list after creation
    }
}
```

3. Creating Views

Views render the data for users and provide forms for user input. ASP.NET Core MVC supports Razor syntax for creating dynamic views.

Example: Index.cshtml for Orders

```html
html
Copy code
@model IEnumerable<OrderDto>

<h2>Orders</h2>
<table>
    <thead>
        <tr>
            <th>Order ID</th>
            <th>Total</th>
            <th>Order Date</th>
        </tr>
    </thead>
    <tbody>
        @foreach (var order in Model)
        {
            <tr>
                <td>@order.Id</td>
                <td>@order.Total</td>
                <td>@order.OrderDate</td>
            </tr>
```

```
        }
    </tbody>
</table>
```

Example: Create.cshtml for Creating Orders

```html
Copy code
@model PlaceOrderCommand

<h2>Create Order</h2>
<form asp-action="Create" method="post">
    <label for="CustomerId">Customer ID:</label>
    <input asp-for="CustomerId" />

    <label>Order Lines:</label>
    <!-- Form for order lines goes here -->

    <button type="submit">Place Order</button>
</form>
```

Creating RESTful APIs with ASP.NET Core Web API

In addition to a web application, you might want to expose a RESTful API for client applications or third-party services.

1. Setting Up a Web API Project

Follow these steps to create an ASP.NET Core Web API project:

1. **Create a New Project**:

- Select **ASP.NET Core Web Application** in Visual Studio.
- Choose the **API** template.

1. **Configure the Project**:

- In Startup.cs, configure the API services and CORS if needed.

CHAPTER 7: BUILDING THE USER INTERFACE LAYER

```csharp
Copy code
public void ConfigureServices
(IServiceCollection services)
{
    services.AddControllers();
    services.AddScoped
<IOrderService, OrderService>();
    services.AddCors(options =>
    {
        options.AddPolicy("AllowAll",
            builder =>
            {
                builder.AllowAnyOrigin().
AllowAnyMethod().AllowAnyHeader();
            });
    });
}
```

2. Creating API Controllers

API controllers handle HTTP requests for your RESTful services.

Example: OrderApiController

```csharp
Copy code
[ApiController]
[Route("api/[controller]")]
public class OrderApiController : ControllerBase
{
    private readonly IOrderService _orderService;

    public OrderApiController
(IOrderService orderService)
    {
        _orderService = orderService;
    }
```

```csharp
    [HttpGet]
    public IActionResult GetAllOrders()
    {
        var orders = _orderService.GetAllOrders();
        return Ok(orders);
// Return 200 OK with the orders
    }

    [HttpPost]
    public IActionResult PlaceOrder
([FromBody] PlaceOrderCommand command)
    {
        if (!ModelState.IsValid)
        {
            return BadRequest(ModelState); /
/ Return 400 Bad Request if validation fails
        }

        _orderService.PlaceOrder(command);
        return CreatedAtAction
(nameof(GetAllOrders), new
{ /* parameters */ }); // Return 201 Created
    }
}
```

Handling User Input and Validation in the UI Layer

User input is a critical aspect of any application. It's essential to validate inputs to ensure that the data being processed meets the application's requirements.

1. Implementing Model Validation

Use data annotations or a validation library like FluentValidation to enforce rules on your DTOs.

Example: PlaceOrderCommand with Data Annotations

```
csharp
Copy code
```

```
public class PlaceOrderCommand
{
    [Required(ErrorMessage =
"Customer ID is required.")]
    public int CustomerId { get; set; }

    [Required(ErrorMessage =
"Order lines are required.")]
    public List<OrderLineDto>
OrderLines { get; set; }
}
```

2. Validating Inputs in the UI Layer

In your controllers, validate inputs and return appropriate error responses if the validation fails.

Example: Validating in OrderController

```csharp
Copy code
[HttpPost]
public IActionResult Create([FromBody]
 PlaceOrderCommand command)
{
    if (!ModelState.IsValid)
    {
        return BadRequest(ModelState);
// Return validation errors
    }

    _orderService.PlaceOrder(command);
    return CreatedAtAction(nameof(GetOrder),
new { id = orderId }, order);
}
```

Enhancing User Experience (UX)

A positive user experience is essential for any application. Consider the following techniques to enhance UX in your applications:

1. Responsive Design

Ensure that your application is responsive and works well on different devices and screen sizes. Use CSS frameworks like Bootstrap to create a responsive layout.

2. Loading Indicators and Feedback

Provide users with feedback during long-running operations, such as loading indicators or success messages after form submissions.

Example: Loading Indicator in JavaScript

```html
Copy code
<div id="loading" style="display:none;">Loading...</div>
<script>
    function showLoading() {
        document.getElementById('loading').style.display = 'block';
    }
    function hideLoading() {
        document.getElementById('loading').style.display = 'none';
    }
</script>
```

3. User-Friendly Error Handling

Provide clear and helpful error messages for users when something goes wrong. Use custom error pages for common HTTP errors like 404 (Not Found) or 500 (Internal Server Error).

Example: Custom Error Handling Middleware

```csharp
Copy code
public class CustomErrorHandlingMiddleware
{
    private readonly RequestDelegate _next;

    public CustomErrorHandlingMiddleware
```

CHAPTER 7: BUILDING THE USER INTERFACE LAYER

```csharp
(RequestDelegate next)
    {
        _next = next;
    }

    public async Task Invoke
(HttpContext context)
    {
        try
        {
            await _next(context);
        }
        catch (Exception ex)
        {
            // Log the error
            context.Response.StatusCode =
            (int)HttpStatusCode.InternalServerError;
            await context.Response.
WriteAsync("An unexpected error occurred.
 Please try again.");
        }
    }
}
```

Testing the User Interface Layer

Testing the UI Layer is crucial to ensure that the application behaves as expected and provides a good user experience.

1. Unit Testing Controllers

Unit tests can verify that controllers handle requests correctly and interact with the application layer as expected.

Example: Unit Test for OrderController

```csharp
Copy code
[Fact]
public void Create_ShouldReturnBadRequest
_WhenInvalidModel()
```

```csharp
{
    // Arrange
    var mockService = new Mock<IOrderService>();
    var controller = new OrderController(mockService.Object);
    controller.ModelState.AddModelError("CustomerId", "Customer ID is required.");

    // Act
    var result = controller.Create(new PlaceOrderCommand());

    // Assert
    Assert.IsType<BadRequestObjectResult>(result);
}
```

2. Integration Testing the API

Integration tests can verify that the entire application stack works correctly, including routing and data access.

Example: Integration Test for OrderApiController

```csharp
[Fact]
public async Task PlaceOrder_ShouldReturnCreated_WhenValid()
{
    // Arrange
    var client = _factory.CreateClient();
    var command = new PlaceOrderCommand { /* initialize properties */ };

    // Act
    var response = await client.PostAsJsonAsync("/api/order", command);
```

CHAPTER 7: BUILDING THE USER INTERFACE LAYER

```
    // Assert
    response.StatusCode.Should().
Be(HttpStatusCode.Created);
}
```

Best Practices for the User Interface Layer

1. **Maintain Separation of Concerns**: Keep UI logic separate from application logic. Use controllers to mediate between views and application services.
2. **Use DTOs for Data Transfer**: Use Data Transfer Objects (DTOs) to simplify data exchange between the UI Layer and Application Layer. This helps in managing the data structure effectively.
3. **Implement Validation Early**: Validate user input as early as possible to prevent invalid data from being processed.
4. **Focus on User Experience**: Ensure that the UI is responsive and provides clear feedback to users. Invest time in designing a user-friendly interface.
5. **Automate UI Tests**: Implement automated UI tests using frameworks like Selenium or Playwright to ensure that the application behaves as expected.
6. **Consistent Error Handling**: Provide consistent error handling across the application to improve user experience and maintainability.

Conclusion

The User Interface Layer is a vital component of Clean Architecture, serving as the entry point for users to interact with the application. By implementing effective UI patterns, using ASP.NET Core MVC and Web API, and following best practices, developers can create a responsive and user-friendly interface that adheres to Clean Architecture principles.

In this chapter, we explored the key concepts of the User Interface Layer, including controller implementations, view rendering, API design, and user experience considerations. In the next chapter, we will discuss testing strategies for the entire application, focusing on unit tests, integration tests, and end-to-end tests to ensure the quality and reliability of the system.

Chapter 8: Testing Strategies in Clean Architecture

Introduction
- Overview of the importance of testing in software development.
- Explanation of how testing fits into the Clean Architecture paradigm.
- Discussion on different types of testing and their purposes.

Understanding the Role of Testing in Clean Architecture

Testing is a critical component of software development that ensures the reliability, functionality, and quality of an application. In the context of Clean Architecture, testing plays a vital role in maintaining the integrity of the different layers while allowing for changes and enhancements over time.

Key Benefits of Testing in Clean Architecture:

1. **Verification of Business Logic**: Tests ensure that the core business rules implemented in the Domain Layer behave as expected.
2. **Confidence in Refactoring**: A robust suite of tests allows developers to refactor code with confidence, knowing that any regressions will be caught early.
3. **Documentation**: Tests can serve as documentation for the expected be-

havior of the system, helping new developers understand how different components interact.
4. **Improved Design**: Writing tests often leads to better design choices, as it encourages developers to write more modular, decoupled code.

Types of Testing in Clean Architecture

There are various types of tests that can be implemented within a Clean Architecture application. Each type serves a distinct purpose and targets different layers of the application.

1. Unit Testing

Unit tests focus on testing individual components or methods in isolation. They verify that each unit of code performs as expected.

Characteristics of Unit Tests:

- Fast to execute.
- Should not depend on external systems (like databases or APIs).
- Typically use mocks or stubs to simulate dependencies.

Writing Unit Tests for the Domain Layer

The Domain Layer contains the core business logic, making it essential to have comprehensive unit tests for entities, value objects, and domain services.

Example: Unit Test for the Order Entity

```csharp
Copy code
using Xunit;

public class OrderTests
{
    [Fact]
    public void AddOrderLine_ShouldIncreaseOrderTotal()
    {
        // Arrange
```

```
            var order = new Order(DateTime.UtcNow);
            var product = new Product
(1, "Test Product", 10.00m);

            // Act
            order.AddOrderLine(product, 2);

            // Assert
            Assert.Equal(20.00m, order.Total);
        }

        [Fact]
        public void AddOrderLine_ShouldThrow
_WhenQuantityIsZero()
        {
            // Arrange
            var order = new Order(DateTime.UtcNow);
            var product = new Product
(1, "Test Product", 10.00m);

            // Act & Assert
            var exception = Assert.Throws
<InvalidOperationException>(() =>
order.AddOrderLine(product, 0));
            Assert.Equal
("Quantity must be greater than zero.
", exception.Message);
        }
}
```

2. Integration Testing

Integration tests verify that different parts of the application work together correctly. They typically involve multiple layers, such as the Application Layer and Infrastructure Layer.

Characteristics of Integration Tests:

- Test interactions between components (e.g., API to database).
- Can be slower than unit tests due to external dependencies.

- Focus on the overall behavior of the application.

Writing Integration Tests for the Repository

Integration tests for repositories ensure that data access logic works as intended.

Example: Integration Test for SqlOrderRepository

```csharp
using Microsoft.EntityFrameworkCore;
using Xunit;

public class SqlOrderRepositoryTests
{
    [Fact]
    public void Add_ShouldSaveOrderToDatabase()
    {
        // Arrange
        var options = new DbContextOptionsBuilder<OrderContext>()
            .UseInMemoryDatabase("TestDatabase")
            .Options;

        using (var context = new OrderContext(options))
        {
            var repository = new SqlOrderRepository(context);
            var order = new Order(DateTime.UtcNow);
            order.AddOrderLine(new Product(1, "Test Product", 10.00m), 2);

            // Act
            repository.Add(order);
        }

        // Assert
        using (var context = new OrderContext(options))
        {
```

```
            var savedOrder =
context.Orders.Include
(o => o.OrderLines).FirstOrDefault();
Assert.NotNull(savedOrder);
Assert.Equal(2,
savedOrder.OrderLines.Count);
        }
    }
}
```

3. End-to-End Testing

End-to-end (E2E) tests verify the complete functionality of the application from the user's perspective. They simulate real user scenarios and interactions.

Characteristics of End-to-End Tests:

- Test the application as a whole, including UI and backend interactions.
- Can be time-consuming and fragile due to reliance on external factors.
- Often use tools like Selenium, Cypress, or Playwright.

Writing End-to-End Tests

End-to-end tests can validate user interactions through the UI. Here's how you might set one up:

Example: Using Selenium for E2E Testing

```csharp
csharp
Copy code
using OpenQA.Selenium;
using OpenQA.Selenium.Chrome;
using Xunit;

public class OrderEndToEndTests : IDisposable
{
    private readonly IWebDriver _driver;
```

```csharp
    public OrderEndToEndTests()
    {
        _driver = new ChromeDriver();
    }

    [Fact]
    public void CreateOrder_
ShouldDisplayOrderInList()
    {
        // Arrange
        _driver.Navigate().GoToUrl
("http://localhost:5000/Order/Create");
        _driver.FindElement(By.Id
("CustomerId")).SendKeys("1");
        _driver.FindElement(By.Id
("OrderLines_0__ProductId")).SendKeys("1");
        _driver.FindElement(By.Id(
"OrderLines_0__Quantity")).SendKeys("2");
        _driver.FindElement(By.CssSelector
("button[type='submit']")).Click();

        // Act
        _driver.Navigate().GoToUrl
("http://localhost:5000/Order/Index");

        // Assert
        var orderTable = _driver.FindElement(By.Id("ordersTable"));
        Assert.Contains
("Order Total", orderTable.Text);
    }

    public void Dispose()
    {
        _driver.Quit();
    }
}
```

Best Practices for Testing in Clean Architecture

1. **Keep Tests Independent**: Each test should run independently of others.

CHAPTER 8: TESTING STRATEGIES IN CLEAN ARCHITECTURE

Avoid sharing state between tests to prevent flaky behavior.
2. **Use Mocks and Stubs**: For unit tests, use mocking frameworks like Moq or NSubstitute to isolate components and test them in isolation.
3. **Test Coverage**: Aim for a high level of test coverage, particularly for critical business logic in the Domain Layer.
4. **Automate Testing**: Integrate tests into your Continuous Integration (CI) pipeline to ensure that tests run automatically with each code change.
5. **Focus on Behavior**: Write tests that verify the behavior of the system rather than the implementation details. This encourages better design and reduces fragility.
6. **Use Meaningful Assertions**: Make sure assertions provide clear information about the failure. This helps in quickly diagnosing issues when tests fail.
7. **Regularly Review and Refactor Tests**: Just like application code, tests can become outdated or bloated. Regularly review and refactor tests to keep them relevant and effective.

Testing Strategies for the Application Layer

In the context of Clean Architecture, the Application Layer is where many interactions occur. Therefore, it's crucial to have a comprehensive testing strategy for this layer.

1. Testing Command Handlers

Command handlers contain the business logic to process commands. Unit tests for command handlers should verify that the expected actions occur and that the application state is correct after the command is processed.

Example: Unit Test for PlaceOrderHandler

```csharp
Copy code
using Moq;
using Xunit;
```

```csharp
public class PlaceOrderHandlerTests
{
    [Fact]
    public void Handle_ShouldAddOrder_WhenValidCommand()
    {
        // Arrange
        var mockRepository = new Mock<IOrderRepository>();
        var handler = new PlaceOrderHandler(mockRepository.Object);
        var command = new PlaceOrderCommand { /* initialize
        properties */ };

        // Act
        handler.Handle(command);

        // Assert
        mockRepository.Verify(r => r.Add(It.IsAny<Order>()),
        Times.Once);
    }

    [Fact]
    public void Handle_ShouldThrow_WhenCommandIsInvalid()
    {
        // Arrange
        var mockRepository = new Mock<IOrderRepository>();
        var handler = new PlaceOrderHandler(mockRepository.Object);
        var command = new PlaceOrderCommand { /* initialize with
        invalid data */ };

        // Act & Assert
        Assert.Throws<ValidationException>(() =>
        handler.Handle(command));
    }
}
```

2. Testing Query Handlers

Query handlers retrieve data and should be tested to ensure that they return the expected results.

Example: Unit Test for GetOrderDetailsQueryHandler

CHAPTER 8: TESTING STRATEGIES IN CLEAN ARCHITECTURE

```csharp
Copy code
using Moq;
using Xunit;

public class GetOrderDetailsQueryHandlerTests
{
    [Fact]
    public void Handle_ShouldReturnOrderDetails_WhenOrderExists()
    {
        // Arrange
        var mockRepository = new Mock<IOrderRepository>();
        var handler = new GetOrderDetailsQueryHandler(mockRepository.Object);
        var order = new Order { Id = 1, /* other properties */ };
        mockRepository.Setup(r => r.GetById(1)).Returns(order);

        // Act
        var result = handler.Handle(new GetOrderDetailsQuery { OrderId = 1 });

        // Assert
        Assert.NotNull(result);
        Assert.Equal(1, result.Id);
    }

    [Fact]
    public void Handle_ShouldThrow_WhenOrderDoesNotExist()
    {
        // Arrange
        var mockRepository = new Mock<IOrderRepository>();
        var handler = new GetOrderDetailsQueryHandler(mockRepository.Object);
        mockRepository.Setup(r => r.GetById(1)).Returns((Order)null);

        // Act & Assert
        Assert.Throws<NotFoundException>(() => handler.Handle(new GetOrderDetailsQuery { OrderId = 1 }));
    }
```

}

Testing Strategies for the Domain Layer

The Domain Layer is the core of the application and should have thorough test coverage to ensure the business rules are correctly implemented.

1. Testing Entities and Value Objects

Unit tests for entities and value objects should validate that the properties and methods behave as expected, including enforcing invariants.

Example: Unit Test for Money Value Object

```csharp
Copy code
using Xunit;

public class MoneyTests
{
    [Fact]
    public void Constructor_ShouldThrow_WhenNegativeAmount()
    {
        // Act & Assert
        Assert.Throws<ArgumentOutOfRangeException>(() => new Money(-1, "USD"));
    }

    [Fact]
    public void OperatorPlus_ShouldAddSameCurrency()
    {
        // Arrange
        var money1 = new Money(10, "USD");
        var money2 = new Money(5, "USD");

        // Act
        var result = money1 + money2;

        // Assert
        Assert.Equal(15, result.Amount);
        Assert.Equal("USD", result.Currency);
    }
```

CHAPTER 8: TESTING STRATEGIES IN CLEAN ARCHITECTURE

```csharp
    [Fact]
    public void OperatorPlus_ShouldThrow_WhenDifferentCurrencies()
    {
        // Arrange
        var money1 = new Money(10, "USD");
        var money2 = new Money(5, "EUR");

        // Act & Assert
        Assert.Throws<InvalidOperationException>(() => money1 +
        money2);
    }
}
```

2. Testing Domain Services

Domain services that encapsulate business logic spanning multiple entities should be thoroughly tested to ensure their correctness.

Example: Unit Test for OrderProcessingService

```
csharp
Copy code
using Moq;
using Xunit;

public class OrderProcessingServiceTests
{
    [Fact]
    public void ProcessOrder_ShouldChargePayment()
    {
        // Arrange
        var mockRepository = new Mock<IOrderRepository>();
        var mockPaymentGateway = new Mock<IPaymentGateway>();
        var service = new
        OrderProcessingService(mockRepository.Object,
        mockPaymentGateway.Object);
        var order = new Order(DateTime.UtcNow);

        // Act
```

```
        service.ProcessOrder(order);

        // Assert
        mockPaymentGateway.Verify(g =>
            g.Charge(It.IsAny<Money>()), Times.Once);
    }
}
```

Conclusion

Testing is an integral part of developing applications following Clean Architecture principles. By implementing unit tests, integration tests, and end-to-end tests, developers can ensure the reliability and functionality of their applications.

In this chapter, we have covered various testing strategies for the different layers of the application, focusing on unit tests for individual components, integration tests for interactions between components, and end-to-end tests for user scenarios. We also discussed best practices to create an effective testing strategy.

In the next chapter, we will explore the deployment strategies for Clean Architecture applications, including containerization, cloud deployment, and CI/CD pipelines.

Chapter 9: Deployment Strategies in Clean Architecture

Introduction
- Overview of deployment strategies and their importance in the software development lifecycle.
- Explanation of how deployment fits into Clean Architecture.
- Discussion of the benefits of having a well-defined deployment strategy, including improved reliability, scalability, and maintainability.

Understanding the Deployment Process

Deployment is the process of making a software application available for use. This can involve installing, configuring, and enabling an application on a server or cloud environment. A robust deployment strategy is critical for ensuring that the application operates correctly in production environments.

Key Goals of Deployment:

1. **Reliability**: Ensure that the application is stable and operates as intended.
2. **Scalability**: Design deployment processes that can accommodate increased loads or user demand.

3. **Automation**: Minimize manual steps to reduce errors and improve efficiency.
4. **Security**: Protect the application and its data during deployment.

Containerization with Docker

Containerization is a method of packaging applications and their dependencies into a standardized unit called a container. Docker is one of the most popular tools for creating and managing containers.

1. Benefits of Containerization

- **Consistency**: Containers encapsulate the application and its environment, ensuring it runs the same way across different environments (development, testing, production).
- **Isolation**: Each container runs in its own environment, preventing conflicts with other applications.
- **Portability**: Containers can be easily moved across different infrastructures, whether on-premises or in the cloud.

2. Setting Up Docker for a .NET Application

To deploy a .NET application using Docker, you will need to create a Dockerfile that defines how to build the application container.

Creating a Dockerfile

1. **Create a New File**: In the root of your project, create a file named Dockerfile.
2. **Define the Dockerfile**:

```dockerfile
Copy code
# Use the official ASP.NET Core runtime as a base image
FROM mcr.microsoft.com/dotnet/aspnet:5.0 AS base
WORKDIR /app
```

CHAPTER 9: DEPLOYMENT STRATEGIES IN CLEAN ARCHITECTURE

```
EXPOSE 80

# Use the SDK image for building the application
FROM mcr.microsoft.com/dotnet/sdk:5.0 AS build
WORKDIR /src
COPY ["OrderManagementUI/OrderManagementUI.csproj",
"OrderManagementUI/"]
RUN dotnet restore "OrderManagementUI
/OrderManagementUI.csproj"
COPY . .
WORKDIR "/src/OrderManagementUI"
RUN dotnet build "OrderManagementUI.csproj"
 -c Release -o /app/build

# Publish the application
FROM build AS publish
RUN dotnet publish
"OrderManagementUI.csproj"
-c Release -o /app/publish

# Final stage: Build the runtime image
FROM base AS final
WORKDIR /app
COPY --from=publish /app/publish .
ENTRYPOINT ["dotnet", "OrderManagementUI.dll"]
```

3. Building the Docker Image

To build the Docker image for your application, run the following command from the terminal in the directory containing your Dockerfile:

```bash
Copy code
docker build -t order-management-ui .
```

4. Running the Docker Container

Once the image is built, you can run it using the following command:

```bash
Copy code
docker run -d -p 8080:80
--name order-management-ui
order-management-ui
```

This command runs the container in detached mode (-d) and maps port 8080 on your host to port 80 in the container.

Deploying to the Cloud

Cloud computing platforms provide scalable resources and services for deploying applications. Common platforms include Microsoft Azure, Amazon Web Services (AWS), and Google Cloud Platform (GCP).

1. Deploying to Microsoft Azure

Azure provides several services for deploying .NET applications, including Azure App Service, Azure Kubernetes Service (AKS), and Azure Container Instances.

Deploying to Azure App Service

1. **Create an Azure App Service**: In the Azure portal, create a new App Service and configure it for .NET 5.
2. **Publish from Visual Studio**:

- Right-click the project in Solution Explorer and select **Publish**.
- Choose **Azure** as the target and select the Azure App Service you created.
- Configure settings and publish the application.

Using Azure DevOps for CI/CD

1. **Create a New Azure DevOps Project**: In Azure DevOps, create a new project to host your CI/CD pipelines.
2. **Set Up a Build Pipeline**: Configure a build pipeline to automate the build process using a Dockerfile.
3. **Set Up a Release Pipeline**: Create a release pipeline to deploy your

application to Azure App Service automatically.

Example: YAML Build Pipeline for Docker

```yaml
Copy code
trigger:
- main

pool:
  vmImage: 'ubuntu-latest'

steps:
- task: Docker@2
  inputs:
    command: 'buildAndPush'
    containerRegistry: 'myContainerRegistry'
    repository: 'order-management-ui'
    dockerfile: '**/Dockerfile'
    tags: '$(Build.BuildId)'
```

2. Deploying to AWS

AWS offers various services for deploying .NET applications, including Elastic Beanstalk, ECS (Elastic Container Service), and EKS (Elastic Kubernetes Service).

Deploying to Elastic Beanstalk

1. **Create an Elastic Beanstalk Application**: In the AWS Management Console, create a new Elastic Beanstalk application and environment.
2. **Deploy Using the Elastic Beanstalk CLI**: Install the EB CLI and use it to deploy your application.

```bash
Copy code
```

```
eb init -p docker order-management-ui
eb create order-env
eb deploy
```

3. Deploying to Google Cloud Platform

GCP provides various services for deploying applications, including Google App Engine, Google Kubernetes Engine (GKE), and Cloud Run.

Deploying to Cloud Run

1. **Install the Google Cloud SDK**: Install the gcloud command-line tool.
2. **Build and Deploy Using gcloud**:

```bash
Copy code
gcloud builds submit --tag gcr.io/[PROJECT_ID]/order-management-ui
gcloud run deploy order-management-ui --image gcr.io/[PROJECT_ID]/order-management-ui --platform managed
```

Continuous Integration and Continuous Deployment (CI/CD)

CI/CD practices automate the process of integrating code changes and deploying applications. Implementing CI/CD helps ensure that your application is continuously tested, built, and deployed, leading to more reliable software delivery.

1. Setting Up CI/CD Pipelines

You can set up CI/CD pipelines using various tools such as Azure DevOps, GitHub Actions, Jenkins, or GitLab CI. These pipelines automate the building, testing, and deployment processes.

Example: GitHub Actions for CI/CD

1. **Create a .github/workflows Directory**: In your repository, create a directory for workflows.

CHAPTER 9: DEPLOYMENT STRATEGIES IN CLEAN ARCHITECTURE

2. **Add a CI Workflow**: Create a YAML file for the CI workflow, specifying the steps for building and testing the application.

Example: CI Workflow

```yaml
Copy code
name: CI

on:
  push:
    branches:
      - main

jobs:
  build:
    runs-on: ubuntu-latest

    steps:
    - name: Checkout code
      uses: actions/checkout@v2

    - name: Set up .NET
      uses: actions/setup-dotnet@v1
      with:
        dotnet-version: '5.0.x'

    - name: Restore dependencies
      run: dotnet restore

    - name: Build
      run: dotnet build --configuration Release

    - name: Run tests
      run: dotnet test --configuration Release
```

Example: CD Workflow for Docker Deployment

1. **Add a CD Workflow**: Create a separate YAML file for the CD workflow

to deploy the application.

Example: CD Workflow

```yaml
Copy code
name: CD

on:
  push:
    branches:
      - main

jobs:
  deploy:
    runs-on: ubuntu-latest

    steps:
    - name: Checkout code
      uses: actions/checkout@v2

    - name: Build Docker image
      run: |
        docker build -t mycontainerregistry/order-management-ui .

    - name: Push Docker image
      run: |
        echo "${{ secrets.DOCKER_PASSWORD }}" | docker login -u "${{ secrets.DOCKER_USERNAME }}" --password-stdin
        docker push mycontainerregistry/order-management-ui

    - name: Deploy to Azure
      run: |
        az webapp update --name my-app --resource-group my-resource-group --docker-image
```

CHAPTER 9: DEPLOYMENT STRATEGIES IN CLEAN ARCHITECTURE

```
mycontainerregistry/
order-management-ui
```

2. Monitoring and Logging in Production

Once deployed, it's crucial to monitor your application and capture logs to identify issues proactively.

Using Application Insights

Integrate Azure Application Insights or a similar service to monitor application performance and errors in real-time.

1. **Add Application Insights to Your Application**:

- Install the required NuGet packages.
- Configure Application Insights in Startup.cs.

```csharp
Copy code
public void ConfigureServices
(IServiceCollection services)
{
    services.AddApplicationInsightsTelemetry
(Configuration[
"ApplicationInsights:
InstrumentationKey"]);
}
```

1. **Monitor Application Health**: Use Application Insights to track requests, dependencies, exceptions, and performance metrics.

Scaling and Load Balancing

As your application grows, it's essential to plan for scalability. Scalability refers to the ability of the application to handle increased load or traffic.

1. Horizontal vs. Vertical Scaling

- **Horizontal Scaling**: Involves adding more instances of the application (e.g., more servers or containers) to distribute the load.
- **Vertical Scaling**: Involves upgrading the existing server resources (e.g., more CPU, RAM).

2. Implementing Load Balancing

Use load balancers to distribute incoming traffic across multiple instances of your application, improving performance and reliability.

Using Azure Load Balancer

In Azure, you can set up a load balancer to distribute traffic to multiple instances of your application running on Azure App Service or VMs.

1. **Create an Azure Load Balancer**: In the Azure portal, create a new load balancer and configure it to point to your application instances.
2. **Configure Load Balancing Rules**: Set up rules to determine how traffic should be distributed.

Using AWS Elastic Load Balancing

In AWS, use Elastic Load Balancing to automatically distribute incoming application traffic across multiple targets.

1. **Create a Load Balancer**: In the AWS Management Console, create a new load balancer.
2. **Configure Target Groups**: Define target groups for your application instances.

Best Practices for Deployment in Clean Architecture

1. **Automate Everything**: Automate your build, testing, and deployment processes to reduce human error and increase efficiency.
2. **Use Infrastructure as Code (IaC)**: Utilize tools like Terraform or Azure Resource Manager (ARM) templates to manage your infrastructure declaratively.

3. **Implement Rollback Strategies**: Ensure that you have rollback strategies in place to revert to a previous stable version in case of deployment failures.
4. **Test in Production**: Use techniques like blue-green deployments or canary releases to test new features with a subset of users before a full rollout.
5. **Monitor Post-Deployment**: Implement monitoring and alerting to track application health and performance after deployment.
6. **Document Your Deployment Processes**: Maintain documentation for your deployment procedures, including steps for troubleshooting and recovery.

Conclusion

Deployment is a critical aspect of software development that can significantly impact the success of an application. In this chapter, we explored various deployment strategies, including containerization, cloud deployment, and CI/CD practices. We also discussed scaling, load balancing, and best practices for ensuring a smooth and reliable deployment process.

With a solid deployment strategy in place, your application can achieve the scalability, reliability, and maintainability necessary to thrive in production environments. In the next chapter, we will discuss advanced topics, including implementing security measures and handling data migrations within the context of Clean Architecture.

Chapter 10: Security in Clean Architecture

Introduction
- Overview of the importance of security in software development.
- Explanation of how security fits into the Clean Architecture framework.
- Discussion of the potential risks and vulnerabilities associated with modern applications.

Understanding Security in Clean Architecture

Security should be an integral part of the software development lifecycle rather than an afterthought. In Clean Architecture, security concerns must be addressed at each layer of the application, ensuring that all components are adequately protected.

Key Goals of Security in Clean Architecture:

1. **Data Protection**: Safeguarding sensitive data from unauthorized access and breaches.
2. **Authentication**: Verifying the identity of users or systems attempting to access the application.
3. **Authorization**: Ensuring that authenticated users have appropriate

permissions to perform actions.
4. **Secure Communication**: Protecting data in transit between clients and servers.

Securing the Application

To ensure the security of an application built using Clean Architecture, developers must implement various security measures at different layers.

1. Securing the User Interface Layer

The User Interface Layer is the entry point for users, making it essential to enforce security measures here.

a. Input Validation

Implement input validation to prevent attacks such as SQL injection and cross-site scripting (XSS).

- **Example**: Validate all user inputs on the server-side and use built-in validation features provided by frameworks.

ASP.NET Core Data Annotations for Validation

```csharp
Copy code
public class UserRegistrationCommand
{
    [Required]
    [EmailAddress]
    public string Email { get; set; }

    [Required]
    [StringLength(100, MinimumLength = 6)]
    public string Password { get; set; }
}
```

b. Output Encoding

Use output encoding to protect against XSS attacks by ensuring that any data rendered in views is safely encoded.

Example: Using Razor to Encode Output

```html
Copy code
@Html.Encode(Model.UserInput)
// This ensures that user input is
safely encoded before rendering
```

c. Secure Cookies and Session Management

Ensure cookies are marked as HttpOnly and Secure to protect against session hijacking.

Example: Configuring Cookie Settings in ASP.NET Core

```csharp
Copy code
services.ConfigureApplicationCookie(options =>
{
    options.Cookie.HttpOnly = true;
    options.Cookie.SecurePolicy = CookieSecurePolicy.Always;
    options.SlidingExpiration = true;
});
```

2. Implementing Authentication and Authorization

Proper authentication and authorization mechanisms are crucial for securing applications.

a. Authentication

Authentication verifies the identity of users. Common authentication methods include:

- **Username and Password**: The most traditional method, requiring users to enter credentials.
- **OAuth2**: An industry-standard protocol for authorization, commonly used to allow third-party applications to access user data without exposing credentials.
- **OpenID Connect**: An identity layer on top of OAuth2, allowing for user

authentication.

Example: ASP.NET Core Identity for Authentication

1. **Install Required Packages**:

```bash
Copy code
Install-Package Microsoft.AspNetCore.Identity.EntityFrameworkCore
```

1. **Configure Identity in Startup.cs**:

```csharp
Copy code
public void ConfigureServices(IServiceCollection services)
{
    services.AddDbContext<ApplicationDbContext>(options =>
        options.UseSqlServer(Configuration.GetConnectionString("DefaultConnection")));

    services.AddIdentity<ApplicationUser, IdentityRole>()
        .AddEntityFrameworkStores<ApplicationDbContext>()
        .AddDefaultTokenProviders();
}
```

1. **Create a Registration Endpoint**:

```csharp
Copy code
[HttpPost]
public async Task<IActionResult> Register([FromBody] UserRegistrationCommand command)
{
    var user = new ApplicationUser { UserName = command.Email, Email = command.Email };
    var result = await _userManager.CreateAsync(user, command.Password);

    if (!result.Succeeded)
    {
        return BadRequest(result.Errors);
    }

    return Ok();
}
```

b. Authorization

Authorization determines what authenticated users can do. Use role-based or policy-based authorization to control access.

Example: Role-Based Authorization

```csharp
Copy code
[Authorize(Roles = "Admin")]
public class AdminController : Controller
{
    public IActionResult Index()
    {
        return View();
    }
}
```

c. Token-Based Authentication

CHAPTER 10: SECURITY IN CLEAN ARCHITECTURE

For APIs, implement token-based authentication, such as JWT (JSON Web Tokens).

Example: Configuring JWT Authentication

1. **Install Required Packages**:

```bash
Copy code
Install-Package Microsoft.AspNetCore.Authentication.JwtBearer
```

1. **Configure JWT in Startup.cs**:

```csharp
Copy code
public void ConfigureServices
(IServiceCollection services)
{
    services.AddAuthentication(options =>
    {
        options.DefaultAuthenticateScheme =
        JwtBearerDefaults.AuthenticationScheme;
        options.DefaultChallengeScheme =
        JwtBearerDefaults.AuthenticationScheme;
    })
    .AddJwtBearer(options =>
    {
options.TokenValidationParameters = new TokenValidationParameters
        {
ValidateIssuer = true,
ValidateAudience = true,
ValidateLifetime = true,
ValidateIssuerSigningKey = true,
            // Configure your
```

```
token validation parameters here
        };
    });
}
```

3. Securing the Application Layer

The Application Layer orchestrates interactions between the UI Layer and the Domain Layer, making it vital to enforce security practices.

a. Service Layer Security

Ensure that all service methods validate user permissions before executing any actions.

Example: Authorizing Service Methods

```csharp
Copy code
public class OrderService : IOrderService
{
    private readonly IAuthorizationService _authorizationService;

    public OrderService(IAuthorizationService authorizationService)
    {
        _authorizationService = authorizationService;
    }

    public async Task PlaceOrder(PlaceOrderCommand command, ClaimsPrincipal user)
    {
        var isAuthorized = await _authorizationService.AuthorizeAsync(user, null, "PlaceOrderPolicy");
        if (!isAuthorized.Succeeded)
        {
            throw new UnauthorizedAccessException("You are not authorized to place an order.");
        }
```

CHAPTER 10: SECURITY IN CLEAN ARCHITECTURE

```csharp
    // Proceed with placing the order...
    }
}
```

b. Validation and Error Handling

Implement input validation and robust error handling in your application services to protect against malformed requests and provide meaningful feedback to users.

Example: Validating Input in Application Services

```csharp
Copy code
public void PlaceOrder(PlaceOrderCommand command)
{
    if (string.IsNullOrWhiteSpace
(command.CustomerId.ToString()))
    {
        throw new ArgumentException("Customer ID is required.");
    }

    // Process the order...
}
```

4. Securing the Infrastructure Layer

The Infrastructure Layer handles data access and external service interactions. It is essential to secure these components to protect sensitive data and maintain integrity.

a. Secure Data Access

Ensure that data access is performed securely by using parameterized queries or ORM features to prevent SQL injection.

Example: Using Entity Framework Core with Parameterization

```csharp
Copy code
```

```
public async Task<Order> GetOrderByIdAsync(int id)
{
    return await _context.Orders.
FindAsync(id); // EF Core handles parameterization internally
}
```

b. Securing External Service Integrations

When integrating with external services, use secure communication methods, such as HTTPS, and authenticate requests using API keys or OAuth tokens.

Example: Using HttpClient with API Keys

```csharp
Copy code
public class ExternalServiceClient
{
    private readonly HttpClient _httpClient;

    public ExternalServiceClient(HttpClient httpClient)
    {
        _httpClient = httpClient;
    }

    public async Task<string> GetDataAsync()
    {
        _httpClient.DefaultRequestHeaders.Authorization = new AuthenticationHeaderValue("Bearer", "your_api_key_here");
        var response = await _httpClient.GetAsync("https://api.external-service.com/data");
        response.EnsureSuccessStatusCode();
        return await response.Content.ReadAsStringAsync();
    }
}
```

Implementing Data Protection

CHAPTER 10: SECURITY IN CLEAN ARCHITECTURE

Data protection is crucial for safeguarding sensitive information, both at rest and in transit.

1. Encrypting Sensitive Data

Implement encryption for sensitive data stored in databases, such as passwords and personal identification information.

a. Hashing Passwords

Use a secure hashing algorithm, such as bcrypt or PBKDF2, to hash passwords before storing them.

Example: Hashing a Password

```csharp
Copy code
public class PasswordHasher
{
    public string HashPassword(string password)
    {
        return BCrypt.Net.BCrypt.HashPassword(password);
    }

    public bool VerifyPassword(string hashedPassword, string providedPassword)
    {
        return BCrypt.Net.BCrypt.Verify(providedPassword, hashedPassword);
    }
}
```

b. Data Encryption at Rest

For sensitive data in databases, consider using encryption features provided by the database system.

Example: SQL Server Transparent Data Encryption (TDE)

- Enable TDE to encrypt database files on SQL Server.

2. Securing Data in Transit

Use HTTPS for secure communication between clients and servers, ensuring data is encrypted in transit.

a. Configuring HTTPS in ASP.NET Core

1. **Enforce HTTPS**: In Startup.cs, configure the application to enforce HTTPS.

```csharp
Copy code
public void Configure(IApplicationBuilder app, IWebHostEnvironment env)
{
    app.UseHttpsRedirection();
    // Other middleware...
}
```

1. **Redirect HTTP to HTTPS**: Use middleware to redirect HTTP requests to HTTPS.

Secure Coding Practices

Adopting secure coding practices is essential for minimizing vulnerabilities and ensuring robust security.

1. Principle of Least Privilege

Grant users the minimum level of access necessary to perform their tasks. This minimizes the risk of unauthorized access or data breaches.

2. Input Sanitization

Always sanitize and validate user inputs to prevent injection attacks.

3. Regular Security Audits

Conduct regular security audits and code reviews to identify and mitigate vulnerabilities.

4. Use Security Libraries and Tools

Leverage existing security libraries and tools to implement common security patterns and practices, such as OWASP's ZAP for vulnerability scanning.

Monitoring and Incident Response

Monitoring the application for security breaches and having an incident response plan is vital for maintaining security.

1. Implement Logging and Monitoring

Integrate logging to capture security-related events, such as authentication attempts and authorization failures.

Using Serilog for Logging

```csharp
Copy code
public void ConfigureServices
(IServiceCollection services)
{
    services.AddLogging(loggingBuilder =>
    {
        loggingBuilder.AddSerilog(
new LoggerConfiguration()
            .MinimumLevel.Information()
            .WriteTo.Console()
            .CreateLogger());
    });
}
```

2. Set Up Alerts

Configure alerts for suspicious activities, such as multiple failed login attempts or access to sensitive data.

3. Develop an Incident Response Plan

Have a clear incident response plan in place to address security breaches, including steps for containment, eradication, recovery, and post-incident analysis.

Conclusion

Security is a critical aspect of developing applications in Clean Architecture. By implementing robust security measures across all layers—User Interface, Application, Domain, and Infrastructure—developers can protect sensitive data, ensure compliance with regulations, and provide a secure user experience.

In this chapter, we explored various security principles and practices, including authentication and authorization, data protection, secure coding practices, and monitoring. With a strong focus on security, your application can achieve resilience against threats and vulnerabilities.

In the next chapter, we will delve into advanced topics such as performance optimization, scalability strategies, and best practices for maintaining a high-performance application.

Chapter 11: Performance Optimization in Clean Architecture

Introduction
- Overview of the significance of performance optimization in software development.
- Explanation of how performance fits into Clean Architecture and its various layers.
- Discussion of the impact of performance on user experience and system scalability.

Understanding Performance in Clean Architecture

Performance optimization involves making adjustments to an application to enhance its speed, responsiveness, and resource efficiency. In Clean Architecture, performance considerations must be applied at each layer while maintaining the principles of separation of concerns and modular design.

Key Goals of Performance Optimization:

1. **Reduced Latency**: Minimize the time it takes for the application to respond to user inputs or service requests.
2. **Efficient Resource Utilization**: Ensure that the application uses memory, CPU, and network resources effectively.

3. **Scalability**: Design the application to handle increased load without degrading performance.
4. **User Satisfaction**: Improve the overall user experience by ensuring that applications respond quickly and efficiently.

Performance Optimization Strategies

1. Optimizing the User Interface Layer

The User Interface Layer is the first point of interaction for users, making it crucial to optimize for performance.

a. Reduce Page Load Times

- **Minimize HTTP Requests**: Combine CSS and JavaScript files, use image sprites, and minimize the number of resources requested.
- **Implement Lazy Loading**: Load images and other resources only when they enter the viewport, reducing initial load times.

Example: Lazy Loading Images

```html
html
Copy code
<img src="placeholder.jpg" data-src="actual-image.jpg" class="lazy" alt="Description" />
<script>
    document.addEventListener("DOMContentLoaded", function () {
        const lazyImages = document.querySelectorAll('.lazy');
        const observer = new IntersectionObserver(entries => {
            entries.forEach(entry => {
                if (entry.isIntersecting) {
                    const img = entry.target;
                    img.src = img.dataset.src;
                    img.classList.remove('lazy');
                    observer.unobserve(img);
                }
            });
        });
        lazyImages.forEach(img => {
```

```
        observer.observe(img);
    });
  });
</script>
```

b. Optimize Rendering Performance

- **Minimize Reflows and Repaints**: Structure your HTML and CSS to reduce the need for the browser to recalculate styles and layouts.
- **Use Efficient CSS Selectors**: Avoid complex selectors that can slow down the rendering process.

c. Reduce JavaScript Execution Time

- **Debounce and Throttle Events**: Optimize event handlers to prevent excessive function calls, especially on scroll and resize events.

Example: Debounce Function

```
javascript
Copy code
function debounce(func, wait) {
    let timeout;
    return function(...args) {
        clearTimeout(timeout);
        timeout = setTimeout(() => func.apply(this, args), wait);
    };
}
```

2. Optimizing the Application Layer

The Application Layer coordinates requests and manages interactions with the Domain Layer. Optimizing this layer is crucial for overall performance.

a. Efficient Command and Query Handling

- **Use CQRS (Command Query Responsibility Segregation)**: Separate commands and queries to optimize read and write operations. This allows for optimized data access strategies.

Example: Implementing CQRS

```csharp
Copy code
public class PlaceOrderCommand { /* Command details */ }
public class GetOrderDetailsQuery { /* Query details */ }

public class CommandHandler
{
    public void Handle(PlaceOrderCommand command)
 { /* Handle command */ }
}

public class QueryHandler
{
    public OrderDto Handle
(GetOrderDetailsQuery query) { /* Handle query */ }
}
```

b. Implement Caching Strategies

Use caching to store frequently accessed data, reducing the need to query the database or perform expensive computations.

Example: Using Memory Cache in ASP.NET Core

```csharp
Copy code
public class OrderService : IOrderService
{
    private readonly IMemoryCache _cache;

    public OrderService(IMemoryCache cache)
    {
        _cache = cache;
    }
```

CHAPTER 11: PERFORMANCE OPTIMIZATION IN CLEAN ARCHITECTURE

```
public OrderDto GetOrder(int orderId)
{
    if (!_cache.TryGetValue(orderId, out OrderDto order))
    {
        order = // fetch from repository
        _cache.Set(orderId, order,
TimeSpan.FromMinutes(10));
// Cache for 10 minutes
    }
    return order;
}
}
```

c. Optimize Database Access

- **Use Asynchronous Data Access**: Leverage asynchronous programming to avoid blocking calls, which can improve responsiveness.

Example: Asynchronous Repository Method

```csharp
Copy code
public async Task<Order> GetOrderByIdAsync(int id)
{
    return await _context.Orders.FindAsync(id);
}
```

- **Batch Database Operations**: Instead of performing multiple round trips to the database, batch operations when possible.

Example: Batch Insert Using EF Core

```csharp
Copy code
public async Task AddOrdersAsync
(IEnumerable<Order> orders)
{
    await _context.Orders.AddRangeAsync(orders);
    await _context.SaveChangesAsync();
}
```

3. Optimizing the Domain Layer

The Domain Layer contains business logic and rules, making it crucial to optimize for performance while maintaining integrity.

a. Avoid Complex Business Logic in the UI

Keep business logic out of the UI Layer to avoid performance bottlenecks. Move any necessary calculations or processing to the Domain Layer.

b. Use Domain Events Wisely

While domain events can help decouple components, be cautious of overusing them, as they can introduce complexity and performance overhead.

Example: Domain Events Handling

```csharp
Copy code
public class OrderPlacedEvent
{
    // Event data
}

public class OrderService
{
    public void PlaceOrder(Order order)
    {
        // Business logic...
        DomainEvents.Raise
(new OrderPlacedEvent(order));
    }
}
```

c. Profiling Domain Logic

Use profiling tools to identify bottlenecks in your domain logic. Optimize algorithms and data structures based on the insights gained.

Example: Profiling with BenchmarkDotNet

```csharp
Copy code
[MemoryDiagnoser]
public class PerformanceTests
{
    [Benchmark]
    public void TestOrderCalculation()
    {
        // Test order calculation logic
    }
}
```

4. Infrastructure Layer Optimization

The Infrastructure Layer deals with data access and external services. Optimizing this layer can significantly enhance overall application performance.

a. Connection Pooling

Use connection pooling to minimize the overhead of establishing database connections.

Example: Configuring Connection Pooling in EF Core

```csharp
Copy code
services.AddDbContext<OrderContext>(options =>
    options.UseSqlServer(Configuration.GetConnectionString("DefaultConnection"),
        sqlOptions => sqlOptions.MaxBatchSize(100));
```

b. Optimize External Service Calls

Minimize the number of external service calls and batch requests when possible. Consider using background jobs for long-running processes.

Example: Using Hangfire for Background Processing

```csharp
Copy code
public void ConfigureServices(IServiceCollection services)
{
    services.AddHangfire(x => x.UseSqlServerStorage(Configuration.GetConnectionString("DefaultConnection")));
    services.AddHangfireServer();
}

public class OrderProcessingService
{
    public void ProcessOrder(Order order)
    {
        BackgroundJob.Enqueue(() => SendConfirmationEmail(order));
    }

    public void SendConfirmationEmail(Order order)
    {
        // Logic to send email
    }
}
```

c. Use Content Delivery Networks (CDNs)

For static assets such as images, CSS, and JavaScript files, use CDNs to reduce latency and improve load times.

Profiling and Monitoring Application Performance

To optimize performance effectively, continuous monitoring and profiling are essential.

1. Application Performance Monitoring (APM) Tools

Use APM tools to monitor application performance in real-time, track requests, and identify bottlenecks.

Popular APM Tools:

- **Azure Application Insights**: Offers telemetry data, including request rates, response times, and failure rates.
- **New Relic**: Provides insights into application performance, user inter-

CHAPTER 11: PERFORMANCE OPTIMIZATION IN CLEAN ARCHITECTURE

actions, and server performance.
- **Dynatrace**: Offers end-to-end monitoring of applications with advanced AI capabilities.

2. Profiling the Application

Use profiling tools to analyze resource consumption and identify performance issues.

Common Profiling Tools:

- **Visual Studio Profiler**: Provides profiling capabilities for .NET applications.
- **DotTrace**: A performance profiler for .NET applications.
- **MiniProfiler**: Lightweight profiling for ASP.NET applications, providing insights into database queries, requests, and response times.

Advanced Performance Techniques

For applications with high scalability requirements, consider implementing advanced performance techniques.

1. Caching Strategies

- **Distributed Caching**: Use distributed cache systems like Redis or Memcached to share cache across multiple instances of your application.
- **Cache Invalidation**: Implement strategies for cache invalidation to ensure that cached data remains accurate and up-to-date.

Example: Configuring Redis Cache in ASP.NET Core

```
csharp
Copy code
services.AddStackExchangeRedisCache(options =>
{
    options.Configuration =
    Configuration.GetConnectionString("RedisConnection");
```

```
});
```

2. Load Testing

Conduct load testing to simulate user demand and identify performance bottlenecks before production deployment.

Using Apache JMeter for Load Testing

1. **Install JMeter**: Download and install Apache JMeter.
2. **Create a Test Plan**: Set up a test plan to simulate concurrent users and measure response times.

Example: Basic JMeter Test Plan

- Add a Thread Group to simulate users.
- Add an HTTP Request Sampler to define requests to the application.
- Add a Listener to visualize results.

Best Practices for Performance Optimization in Clean Architecture

1. **Profile Before Optimizing**: Use profiling tools to identify performance bottlenecks before making changes. Avoid premature optimization.
2. **Keep It Simple**: Strive for simple and maintainable code. Complexity can introduce performance issues and make the application harder to maintain.
3. **Test and Monitor Performance**: Implement automated performance testing as part of your CI/CD pipeline and continuously monitor performance in production.
4. **Optimize Gradually**: Start with high-impact areas and optimize gradually. Measure the performance before and after changes to assess their impact.
5. **Document Performance Considerations**: Maintain documentation on performance optimization strategies and decisions for future reference.

Conclusion

Performance optimization is a crucial aspect of developing applications in Clean Architecture. By implementing effective strategies across all layers—User Interface, Application, Domain, and Infrastructure—developers can enhance responsiveness, scalability, and user satisfaction.

In this chapter, we explored various performance optimization techniques, including strategies for caching, database access, profiling, and monitoring. By following best practices and leveraging appropriate tools, your application can achieve the performance necessary to thrive in production environments.

In the next chapter, we will delve into advanced topics, including implementing security measures and handling data migrations within the context of Clean Architecture.

Chapter 12: Advanced Topics in Clean Architecture

Introduction

- Overview of the advanced topics that will be covered in this chapter.
- Importance of understanding these topics for creating robust and maintainable applications.
- Brief discussion of how these advanced practices complement the foundational principles of Clean Architecture.

Understanding Advanced Architectural Concepts

As applications grow in complexity, advanced architectural concepts become necessary to address common challenges and ensure maintainability, scalability, and security. This chapter will focus on three primary areas: security implementation, data migrations, and architectural patterns that enhance Clean Architecture.

1. Implementing Security Measures

Security is an essential aspect of application development, especially in today's world where threats are increasingly sophisticated. Implementing robust security measures in Clean Architecture requires a comprehensive approach that encompasses various layers of the application.

1.1 Security Best Practices
a. Secure Authentication Mechanisms

- **Multi-Factor Authentication (MFA)**: Implementing MFA to add an additional layer of security beyond just username and password.
- **Use of OAuth2 and OpenID Connect**: Leverage these protocols for secure authentication and authorization, especially for third-party integrations.

Example: Configuring OAuth2 in ASP.NET Core

```csharp
Copy code
services.AddAuthentication(options =>
{
    options.DefaultScheme = JwtBearerDefaults.AuthenticationScheme;
})
.AddJwtBearer(options =>
{
    options.TokenValidationParameters = new
    TokenValidationParameters
    {
        ValidateIssuer = true,
        ValidateAudience = true,
        ValidateLifetime = true,
        ValidateIssuerSigningKey = true,
        // Set your JWT options here
    };
});
```

b. Role-Based Access Control (RBAC)

Implement role-based access control to restrict access to resources based on user roles.

Example: Configuring Roles in ASP.NET Core

```csharp
Copy code
services.AddAuthorization(options =>
{
    options.AddPolicy("AdminOnly", policy =>
        policy.RequireRole("Admin"));
});
```

c. Data Protection

Protect sensitive data in your application by using encryption and hashing.

- **Password Hashing**: Use secure algorithms to hash passwords before storing them in the database.

Example: Hashing Passwords with BCrypt

```csharp
Copy code
public class PasswordHasher
{
    public string HashPassword(string password)
    {
        return BCrypt.Net.BCrypt.HashPassword(password);
    }

    public bool VerifyPassword(string hashedPassword, string providedPassword)
    {
        return BCrypt.Net.BCrypt.Verify(providedPassword, hashedPassword);
    }
}
```

d. Secure Communication

Ensure that data transmitted between clients and servers is encrypted.

- **HTTPS**: Enforce HTTPS to protect data in transit.

Example: Enforcing HTTPS in ASP.NET Core

```csharp
Copy code
public void Configure(IApplicationBuilder app, IWebHostEnvironment env)
{
    app.UseHttpsRedirection();
    // Other middleware
}
```

1.2 Security in the Application Layer

The Application Layer orchestrates the business logic and must ensure that security measures are enforced here.

a. Input Validation and Sanitization

Always validate and sanitize user input to prevent SQL injection and cross-site scripting (XSS) attacks.

Example: Validating Input in the Application Layer

```csharp
Copy code
public void CreateOrder(CreateOrderCommand command)
{
    if (string.IsNullOrWhiteSpace(command.CustomerId))
    {
        throw new ArgumentException("Customer ID cannot be
        empty.");
    }
    // Other validation logic
}
```

b. Logging and Monitoring Security Events

Implement logging for security-related events, such as failed login attempts or unauthorized access attempts.

Example: Using Serilog for Logging Security Events

```csharp
Copy code
Log.ForContext("UserId", userId)
    .Warning("Failed login attempt.");
```

2. Managing Data Migrations

Data migrations are necessary to evolve the database schema over time as the application requirements change. Managing these migrations effectively is crucial to maintaining data integrity and ensuring a smooth upgrade path.

2.1 Using Entity Framework Core Migrations

Entity Framework Core provides a powerful migration feature that helps manage schema changes in a database.

a. Enabling Migrations

1. Install the required NuGet packages for EF Core tools.

```bash
Copy code
Install-Package Microsoft.EntityFrameworkCore.Tools
```

1. Enable migrations using the command line:

```bash
Copy code
Add-Migration InitialCreate
```

b. Applying Migrations

Apply the migrations to update the database schema:

```bash
Copy code
Update-Database
```

2.2 Customizing Migrations

You may need to customize migrations to handle specific scenarios, such as renaming columns or changing data types.

Example: Custom Migration Code

```csharp
Copy code
public partial class RenameColumnInOrders : Migration
{
    protected override void Up(MigrationBuilder migrationBuilder)
    {
        migrationBuilder.RenameColumn(
            name: "OldColumnName",
            table: "Orders",
            newName: "NewColumnName");
    }

    protected override void Down(MigrationBuilder migrationBuilder)
    {
        migrationBuilder.RenameColumn(
            name: "NewColumnName",
            table: "Orders",
            newName: "OldColumnName");
    }
}
```

2.3 Handling Data Seeding

Use migrations to seed initial data into your database.

Example: Seeding Data in Migrations

```csharp
Copy code
protected override void Up(MigrationBuilder migrationBuilder)
{
    migrationBuilder.InsertData(
        table: "Roles",
        columns: new[] { "Id", "Name" },
        values: new object[] { 1, "Admin" });
}
```

2.4 Strategies for Data Migration in Production

When managing migrations in production, consider the following strategies:

1. **Perform Migrations During Off-Peak Hours**: Schedule migrations during periods of low activity to minimize impact.
2. **Test Migrations in Staging Environments**: Always test your migrations in a staging environment before applying them in production.
3. **Use Rollback Plans**: Have rollback plans in case a migration fails to avoid downtime.

3. Architectural Concerns in Clean Architecture

Advanced architectural topics also encompass decisions around how to structure and organize applications to promote maintainability and scalability.

3.1 Microservices Architecture

Microservices architecture breaks an application into small, independent services that can be developed, deployed, and scaled individually. Clean Architecture principles can be applied to each microservice.

a. Benefits of Microservices

- **Scalability**: Each service can be scaled independently based on demand.
- **Resilience**: Failure in one service does not directly impact others.
- **Technology Agnosticism**: Different services can use different technolo-

CHAPTER 12: ADVANCED TOPICS IN CLEAN ARCHITECTURE

gies or languages.

b. Implementing Microservices with Clean Architecture

1. **Define Boundaries**: Clearly define the boundaries of each microservice based on business capabilities.
2. **Decentralized Data Management**: Each microservice should manage its own data and database.
3. **2 Event-Driven Architecture**

Event-driven architecture decouples components through events, enabling asynchronous communication and improving scalability.

a. Implementing Event Sourcing

Event sourcing stores the state of an application as a series of events, allowing for easy tracking of changes.

b. Using Message Brokers

Utilize message brokers like RabbitMQ or Apache Kafka to facilitate communication between services in an event-driven architecture.

Example: Publishing Events Using a Message Broker

```csharp
csharp
Copy code
public async Task PublishOrderCreatedEvent(Order order)
{
    var orderCreatedEvent = new OrderCreatedEvent { OrderId =
    order.Id, OrderTotal = order.Total };
    await _messageBroker.PublishAsync("order.created",
    orderCreatedEvent);
}
```

3.3 Implementing CQRS (Command Query Responsibility Segregation)

CQRS separates the handling of commands (write operations) and queries (read operations), optimizing performance and scalability.

a. Structuring Commands and Queries

- **Commands**: Handle data modifications and enforce business rules.
- **Queries**: Focus on data retrieval and performance optimization.

Example: Command and Query Handlers

```csharp
Copy code
public class PlaceOrderCommand { /* Command details */ }
public class GetOrderDetailsQuery { /* Query details */ }

public class PlaceOrderHandler
{
    public void Handle(PlaceOrderCommand command) { /* Handle
    command logic */ }
}

public class GetOrderDetailsQueryHandler
{
    public OrderDto Handle(GetOrderDetailsQuery query) { /* Handle
    query logic */ }
}
```

Best Practices for Advanced Topics

1. **Keep Security in Mind**: Security should be considered throughout the entire architecture, from the User Interface Layer to the Infrastructure Layer.
2. **Plan for Scalability**: Design your application architecture with scalability in mind, using patterns like microservices or CQRS when appropriate.
3. **Test Thoroughly**: Implement testing strategies for migrations, security, and architectural changes to ensure reliability.
4. **Monitor Performance and Security**: Use monitoring tools to track application performance and detect potential security vulnerabilities in real-time.
5. **Documentation**: Maintain clear documentation for architectural

decisions, security practices, and data migration strategies.

Conclusion

In this chapter, we explored advanced topics within Clean Architecture, including security measures, data migrations, and architectural strategies such as microservices and event-driven architectures. By understanding and implementing these concepts, developers can build robust, scalable, and secure applications that meet the evolving demands of users and businesses.

These advanced practices complement the foundational principles of Clean Architecture, enabling developers to create high-quality software that can adapt to changing requirements. In the next chapter, we will discuss case studies and real-world examples of applying Clean Architecture principles in various scenarios.

Chapter 13: Case Studies and Real-World Applications of Clean Architecture

I ntroduction
- Overview of the importance of case studies in understanding the practical application of Clean Architecture.
- Explanation of how real-world examples can illuminate best practices and potential pitfalls.
- Discussion of the structure of the chapter, including multiple case studies across different industries.

1. Case Study: E-Commerce Platform

1.1 Overview

An e-commerce platform aims to provide users with a seamless shopping experience, including product browsing, shopping cart functionality, and order processing. This case study examines how Clean Architecture principles were applied to create a scalable, maintainable, and secure system.

1.2 Architecture Design

- **Layers**: The architecture consists of four primary layers—UI, Application, Domain, and Infrastructure—each responsible for distinct aspects

CHAPTER 13: CASE STUDIES AND REAL-WORLD APPLICATIONS OF...

of the system.
- **Technologies Used**:
- **Frontend**: React for a responsive UI.
- **Backend**: ASP.NET Core for API development.
- **Database**: SQL Server for data persistence.
- **Caching**: Redis for improving performance.

1.3 Key Features Implemented

- **User Authentication**: Implemented JWT-based authentication for secure user access.
- **Product Management**: Developed a product catalog with advanced search capabilities.
- **Order Processing**: Used CQRS to handle order placement and retrieval efficiently.

1.4 Challenges Faced

- **Scalability**: Initially, the application struggled with scaling during peak shopping times, requiring optimization of database queries and caching strategies.
- **Data Consistency**: Ensuring data consistency across distributed microservices became a challenge, leading to the implementation of eventual consistency patterns.

1.5 Results and Benefits

- **Improved Performance**: Implementing caching and optimizing database queries reduced page load times by over 50%.
- **Enhanced User Experience**: A clean, responsive UI improved user engagement and conversion rates.

2. Case Study: Financial Services Application

2.1 Overview

This case study focuses on a financial services application that provides users with tools for budgeting, expense tracking, and investment management. The system needed to adhere to strict security regulations while offering a seamless user experience.

2.2 Architecture Design

- **Layers**: Similar to the e-commerce platform, this application utilized the Clean Architecture pattern with distinct layers to separate concerns.
- **Technologies Used**:
- **Frontend**: Angular for a dynamic user interface.
- **Backend**: .NET 5 for robust API development.
- **Database**: PostgreSQL for relational data storage.
- **Security**: Implemented Azure Active Directory for user authentication.

2.3 Key Features Implemented

- **Secure User Authentication**: Integrated Azure Active Directory for secure user access and management.
- **Real-Time Data Processing**: Implemented SignalR for real-time updates on financial transactions and account balances.
- **Reporting and Analytics**: Developed reporting features that leverage LINQ for efficient data retrieval and manipulation.

2.4 Challenges Faced

- **Compliance with Regulations**: Ensuring the application met industry regulations such as GDPR required thorough planning and implementation of data protection measures.
- **Performance Issues**: Initial performance tests revealed bottlenecks in data retrieval, prompting the need for query optimization and indexing

strategies.

2.5 Results and Benefits

- **Regulatory Compliance**: The application successfully passed all security audits, ensuring compliance with financial regulations.
- **User Engagement**: Real-time updates improved user engagement and satisfaction, leading to an increase in active users.

3. Case Study: Healthcare Management System

3.1 Overview

This case study examines a healthcare management system designed to streamline patient management, appointment scheduling, and billing processes. The system needed to be secure, user-friendly, and capable of handling sensitive patient information.

3.2 Architecture Design

- **Layers**: Employed Clean Architecture to separate concerns and enhance maintainability.
- **Technologies Used**:
- **Frontend**: Vue.js for an interactive user experience.
- **Backend**: ASP.NET Core Web API for service-oriented architecture.
- **Database**: MySQL for data storage.
- **Data Protection**: Used Azure Key Vault for managing sensitive configuration settings.

3.3 Key Features Implemented

- **Patient Management**: Developed features for managing patient records securely, including appointment history and treatment plans.
- **Role-Based Access Control**: Implemented RBAC to restrict access based on user roles (e.g., doctors, nurses, administrative staff).

- **Billing and Insurance Processing**: Integrated with external APIs for billing and insurance verification.

3.4 Challenges Faced

- **Data Security**: Managing sensitive patient information required stringent data protection measures to comply with HIPAA regulations.
- **Integration with Legacy Systems**: Integrating the new system with existing legacy systems posed compatibility challenges.

3.5 Results and Benefits

- **Improved Efficiency**: Streamlined appointment scheduling and billing processes reduced administrative overhead by 30%.
- **Enhanced Data Security**: Implementing role-based access control and data protection measures ensured compliance with health regulations.

4. Case Study: Social Media Platform

4.1 Overview

This case study focuses on a social media platform that connects users through posts, comments, and messaging. The application requires high availability and responsiveness due to the dynamic nature of social interactions.

4.2 Architecture Design

- **Layers**: Clean Architecture was utilized to maintain a clear separation between UI, application logic, and data management.
- **Technologies Used**:
- **Frontend**: React for a dynamic user interface.
- **Backend**: Node.js with Express for RESTful API development.
- **Database**: MongoDB for handling unstructured data.
- **Real-Time Communication**: Utilized WebSocket for instant messaging

features.

4.3 Key Features Implemented

- **User Profiles**: Developed user profile management capabilities, including settings and preferences.
- **News Feed**: Implemented a real-time news feed that aggregates posts from friends and followed users.
- **Notifications**: Created a notification system for user interactions (likes, comments, messages).

4.4 Challenges Faced

- **Scalability**: The application faced scalability issues during high traffic, necessitating a review of the database schema and the introduction of sharding in MongoDB.
- **Data Consistency**: Managing consistency in a distributed system proved challenging, leading to the adoption of eventual consistency models.

4.5 Results and Benefits

- **Increased User Engagement**: Real-time features and a dynamic UI resulted in a significant increase in user engagement metrics.
- **Scalable Architecture**: Implementing a scalable architecture allowed the platform to handle increased user load without performance degradation.

5. Lessons Learned from Implementing Clean Architecture

5.1 The Importance of Modularity

One of the key benefits observed across all case studies was the modularity afforded by Clean Architecture. This modularity facilitated easier updates and modifications to specific parts of the application without affecting the overall system.

5.2 Emphasis on Security

Security emerged as a critical concern in all projects. Implementing security measures from the outset helped to mitigate risks and ensure compliance with regulations, especially in sensitive industries like healthcare and finance.

5.3 Continuous Improvement and Iteration

All teams emphasized the importance of continuous improvement and iteration. Regular feedback loops, including user testing and performance monitoring, allowed teams to refine their applications continuously.

5.4 Testing as a Core Practice

Thorough testing practices were fundamental to the success of each project. Incorporating unit tests, integration tests, and end-to-end tests helped ensure that the applications were robust and reliable.

5.5 Documentation and Knowledge Sharing

Maintaining clear documentation and fostering a culture of knowledge sharing within teams were crucial for ensuring that all team members understood the architecture and design decisions made throughout the project.

Conclusion

This chapter provided a comprehensive overview of several case studies demonstrating the practical application of Clean Architecture in various domains, including e-commerce, financial services, healthcare, and social media. Each case study illustrated the principles of Clean Architecture in action, highlighting the challenges faced and the benefits achieved.

By analyzing these real-world applications, developers can gain valuable insights into best practices, potential pitfalls, and effective strategies for implementing Clean Architecture in their projects.

The next chapter will focus on future trends and emerging technologies that may impact Clean Architecture, including microservices, serverless computing, and advancements in software development methodologies.

Chapter 14: Future Trends in Clean Architecture

I ntroduction
- Overview of the rapidly changing landscape of software development.
- Explanation of how Clean Architecture provides a solid foundation for adapting to new trends.
- Discussion of the importance of staying current with emerging technologies to maintain competitive advantage.

1. The Rise of Microservices Architecture

1.1 Overview

Microservices architecture is a design approach that structures an application as a collection of small, independently deployable services. Each service is designed around a specific business capability and can be developed, deployed, and scaled independently.

1.2 Benefits of Microservices

- **Scalability**: Each microservice can be scaled independently based on demand, optimizing resource utilization.

- **Resilience**: Failure in one service does not directly impact the overall application, improving fault tolerance.
- **Flexibility in Technology Choices**: Teams can choose the best technologies for each service, enhancing innovation and adaptability.

1.3 Implementing Microservices with Clean Architecture

Integrating microservices with Clean Architecture principles helps maintain separation of concerns while providing the benefits of modularity.

- **Bounded Contexts**: Define bounded contexts for each microservice, ensuring clear boundaries between different business domains.
- **API Communication**: Use lightweight communication protocols, such as REST or gRPC, for interaction between services.

Example: Defining a Bounded Context for an E-Commerce System

- **Order Service**: Manages order placement and tracking.
- **Inventory Service**: Manages stock levels and product availability.
- **User Service**: Handles user profiles, authentication, and authorization.

1.4 Challenges of Microservices

While microservices offer many advantages, they also introduce complexity:

- **Service Coordination**: Managing the communication and orchestration of multiple services can become challenging.
- **Data Management**: Each microservice often manages its own database, requiring strategies for data consistency and integration.

2. Serverless Computing

2.1 Overview

Serverless computing is a cloud computing model where the cloud provider manages the infrastructure, allowing developers to focus solely on writing code. This approach enables automatic scaling and billing based on actual usage rather than pre-allocated resources.

2.2 Benefits of Serverless Computing

- **Cost Efficiency**: Pay only for the compute resources consumed during function execution, reducing operational costs.
- **Automatic Scaling**: Automatically scales based on demand, eliminating the need for manual intervention.
- **Rapid Development**: Allows developers to quickly deploy code without worrying about the underlying infrastructure.

2.3 Integrating Serverless Architecture with Clean Architecture

Serverless functions can align with Clean Architecture by:

- **Decoupling Business Logic**: Use serverless functions for specific business logic, allowing them to evolve independently.
- **Event-Driven Design**: Implement event-driven architectures using serverless functions to respond to events from various sources (e.g., API calls, database changes).

Example: Implementing Serverless Functions in an E-Commerce System

- **Order Processing**: A serverless function that triggers upon new orders to process payments and update inventory.
- **User Notifications**: A serverless function that sends notifications when certain events occur (e.g., order shipped, payment confirmation).

2.4 Challenges of Serverless Computing

Despite its advantages, serverless computing presents some challenges:

- **Cold Start Latency**: Serverless functions may experience latency during cold starts, impacting performance.
- **Limited Execution Time**: Many serverless platforms impose limits on execution time, which may not be suitable for long-running processes.

3. Domain-Driven Design (DDD)

3.1 Overview

Domain-Driven Design is an approach to software development that emphasizes collaboration between technical and domain experts to create a shared understanding of the domain and its complexities. This methodology aligns well with Clean Architecture principles.

3.2 Benefits of DDD

- **Focus on Business Value**: DDD helps ensure that the software aligns closely with business needs and provides real value.
- **Common Language**: Promotes a ubiquitous language among stakeholders, facilitating better communication and understanding.
- **Separation of Concerns**: Encourages the separation of the domain model from technical concerns, aligning well with Clean Architecture.

3.3 Implementing DDD in Clean Architecture

- **Entities and Value Objects**: Define domain entities and value objects that represent core business concepts.
- **Aggregates**: Group related entities into aggregates, enforcing business rules and maintaining invariants.
- **Repositories**: Use repositories to manage aggregates, allowing for easy persistence and retrieval.

Example: DDD Concepts in an E-Commerce Application

- **Order Aggregate**: Composed of Order and OrderLine entities.
- **Product Entity**: Represents products in the inventory, including properties like name, description, and price.

3.4 Challenges of DDD

Implementing DDD can be complex and may require a cultural shift within the organization:

- **Collaboration**: Effective DDD requires collaboration between domain experts and technical teams, which may be challenging in some organizations.
- **Learning Curve**: Teams may face a learning curve in understanding DDD principles and practices.

4. Event-Driven Architecture (EDA)

4.1 Overview

Event-Driven Architecture is a design pattern where the application is structured around events and event handlers. This approach enables asynchronous communication between components and promotes loose coupling.

4.2 Benefits of EDA

- **Scalability**: EDA allows systems to scale more effectively by decoupling components and enabling independent scaling.
- **Flexibility**: Easily accommodate changes in business requirements by adding or modifying event handlers.
- **Resilience**: Event-driven systems can be more resilient to failures, as components can process events independently.

4.3 Integrating EDA with Clean Architecture

Incorporate event-driven design within Clean Architecture by using domain events, event sourcing, and event handlers.

- **Domain Events**: Use domain events to communicate state changes within the application.
- **Event Sourcing**: Store the state of the application as a sequence of events, enabling easy reconstruction of the current state.

Example: Using EDA in an E-Commerce Platform

- **Order Created Event**: When an order is placed, an event is published to notify other components (e.g., inventory, shipping) to react accordingly.
- **Event Handlers**: Implement handlers that listen for specific events and perform necessary actions.

4.4 Challenges of EDA

While EDA offers many benefits, it also introduces complexity:

- **Event Management**: Managing the lifecycle and ordering of events can become challenging.
- **Monitoring**: Monitoring an event-driven system may require specialized tools and strategies to track events and their outcomes.

5. *Continuous Integration and Continuous Deployment (CI/CD)*

5.1 Overview

CI/CD is a set of practices that enable development teams to deliver code changes more frequently and reliably. By integrating code changes regularly and automating deployment processes, teams can improve collaboration and accelerate the development lifecycle.

5.2 Benefits of CI/CD

- **Faster Time to Market**: CI/CD reduces the time required to release

new features and fixes.
- **Increased Quality**: Automated testing and deployment help catch issues early, improving overall code quality.
- **Improved Collaboration**: Teams can work more effectively together, reducing integration issues and conflicts.

5.3 Implementing CI/CD in Clean Architecture

Integrate CI/CD practices into the development workflow to streamline the delivery of Clean Architecture applications.

- **Automated Testing**: Implement automated unit, integration, and end-to-end tests to ensure quality at every stage.
- **Build Automation**: Use tools like Azure DevOps, GitHub Actions, or Jenkins to automate the build process.

Example: CI/CD Pipeline for a .NET Application

1. **Build Stage**: Automatically build the application when code is pushed to the repository.
2. **Test Stage**: Run automated tests to validate functionality.
3. **Deploy Stage**: Deploy the application to a staging environment for further testing and validation before production release.

5.4 Challenges of CI/CD

Implementing CI/CD can present challenges:

- **Complexity of Setup**: Setting up a CI/CD pipeline may require time and expertise, particularly in configuring automated tests and deployment processes.
- **Cultural Shift**: Teams may need to adapt to new workflows and practices, which can be challenging.

6. Observability and Monitoring

6.1 Overview

Observability refers to the ability to monitor and understand the internal state of an application based on the data it generates. This is critical for maintaining performance and quickly diagnosing issues.

6.2 Benefits of Observability

- **Improved Debugging**: Enhanced visibility into application behavior allows teams to identify and resolve issues more effectively.
- **Proactive Performance Management**: Continuous monitoring can help detect performance degradation before it impacts users.
- **Better Decision-Making**: Data-driven insights inform decisions about application improvements and resource allocation.

6.3 Implementing Observability in Clean Architecture

Integrate observability practices into Clean Architecture to enhance monitoring and logging capabilities.

- **Structured Logging**: Use structured logging to capture key events and metrics in a consistent format.

Example: Using Serilog for Structured Logging

```csharp
Copy code
Log.Information("User {UserId}
placed an order {OrderId} at
{Timestamp}", userId, orderId,
 DateTime.UtcNow);
```

- **Metrics Collection**: Collect metrics related to performance, usage, and errors, using tools like Prometheus or Application Insights.

Example: Collecting Metrics with Application Insights

```csharp
Copy code
services.AddApplicationInsightsTelemetry
(Configuration
["ApplicationInsights:
InstrumentationKey"]);
```

6.4 Challenges of Observability

Establishing observability can introduce complexity:

- **Data Overload**: Collecting excessive data can lead to information overload, making it difficult to extract actionable insights.
- **Configuration Management**: Ensuring consistent configuration across services for logging and monitoring can be challenging.

7. Conclusion

As software development continues to evolve, understanding and embracing emerging trends is crucial for building resilient, scalable, and maintainable applications using Clean Architecture. This chapter explored key topics such as microservices, serverless computing, domain-driven design, event-driven architecture, continuous integration and deployment, and observability.

By integrating these advanced practices and technologies, developers can enhance their applications and better meet the demands of users and businesses. The principles of Clean Architecture provide a strong foundation for adopting these trends, ensuring that applications remain flexible and adaptable in a rapidly changing landscape.

In the next chapter, we will summarize the key takeaways from the book and provide guidance on implementing Clean Architecture principles in your projects.

Chapter 15: Implementing Clean Architecture in Real-World Projects

I ntroduction
- Overview of Clean Architecture and its relevance in modern software development.
- Discussion on the importance of a structured approach when implementing Clean Architecture in real-world projects.
- Explanation of the chapter's structure, including step-by-step guides and case study examples.

1. Understanding the Basics of Clean Architecture

1.1 Key Principles

Clean Architecture emphasizes separation of concerns, testability, and maintainability. The key principles include:

- **Independence of Frameworks**: The architecture should not be dependent on any specific framework, allowing flexibility in technology choices.
- **Testability**: The design should facilitate easy testing of individual components.

- **UI Independence**: The user interface can change without affecting the underlying application logic.

1.2 Core Layers of Clean Architecture

- **Entities**: Represent the core business objects and rules.
- **Use Cases/Application Layer**: Contains the application-specific business rules and orchestrates application logic.
- **Interface Adapters**: Handle communication between the application and external systems, such as UI, databases, or third-party APIs.
- **Frameworks and Drivers**: Include the specific tools, frameworks, and libraries used to build the application.

2. Preparing for Implementation

2.1 Assessing Project Requirements

Before implementing Clean Architecture, assess the project's requirements:

- **Understand the Domain**: Gather domain knowledge from stakeholders to ensure that the architecture aligns with business needs.
- **Identify Technical Constraints**: Recognize any existing constraints or dependencies that may affect implementation.

2.2 Planning the Architecture

- **Define Bounded Contexts**: Identify distinct areas of functionality within the application to establish clear boundaries.
- **Design the Layered Structure**: Outline how the application will be structured according to Clean Architecture principles.

3. Step-by-Step Implementation Guide

3.1 Setting Up the Project Structure

Create a solution that follows the layered architecture. Here's a recommended folder structure:

```arduino
Copy code
MyApplication│ ├──
    MyApplication.Core          // Entities and core business logic │ ├──
        Entities │ └──
        Interfaces │ ├──
    MyApplication.Application
            // Use cases and application services │ ├──
        Commands │ └──
        Queries │ ├──
    MyApplication.Infrastructure
            // Data access and external services │ ├──
        Data │ └──
        Services │ └──
    MyApplication.UI
                // User Interface (Web, Mobile, etc.) ├──
        Controllers └──
        Views
```

3.2 Implementing the Core Layer

- **Define Entities**: Create core business entities that reflect the domain model.

Example: Order Entity

CHAPTER 15: IMPLEMENTING CLEAN ARCHITECTURE IN REAL-WORLD...

```csharp
Copy code
public class Order
{
    public int Id { get; private set; }
    public DateTime OrderDate
 { get; private set; }
    public List<OrderLine> OrderLines
{ get; private set; }

    public Order(DateTime orderDate)
    {
        OrderDate = orderDate;
        OrderLines = new List<OrderLine>();
    }

    public void AddOrderLine
(OrderLine orderLine)
    {
        OrderLines.Add(orderLine);
    }
}
```

- **Create Interfaces**: Define repository interfaces for data access.

Example: IOrderRepository Interface

```csharp
Copy code
public interface IOrderRepository
{
    Task<Order> GetByIdAsync(int id);
    Task AddAsync(Order order);
    Task<IEnumerable<Order>> GetAllAsync();
}
```

3.3 Implementing the Application Layer

- **Develop Use Cases**: Create application services that encapsulate specific use cases.

Example: PlaceOrderCommand

```csharp
Copy code
public class PlaceOrderCommand
{
    public int CustomerId { get; set; }
    public List<OrderLineDto> OrderLines { get; set; }
}
```

- **Implement Command Handlers**: Handle business logic within command handlers.

Example: PlaceOrderCommandHandler

```csharp
Copy code
public class PlaceOrderCommandHandler
{
    private readonly IOrderRepository _orderRepository;

    public PlaceOrderCommandHandler(IOrderRepository orderRepository)
    {
        _orderRepository = orderRepository;
    }

    public async Task Handle(PlaceOrderCommand command)
```

CHAPTER 15: IMPLEMENTING CLEAN ARCHITECTURE IN REAL-WORLD...

```
    {
        var order = new Order(DateTime.UtcNow);
        foreach (var line in command.OrderLines)
        {
            order.AddOrderLine
(new OrderLine(line.ProductId, line.Quantity));
        }

        await _orderRepository.AddAsync(order);
    }
}
```

3.4 Implementing the Infrastructure Layer

- **Set Up Data Access**: Implement the repository interfaces to interact with the database.

Example: SqlOrderRepository

```csharp
Copy code
public class SqlOrderRepository : IOrderRepository
{
    private readonly OrderContext _context;

    public SqlOrderRepository
(OrderContext context)
    {
        _context = context;
    }

    public async Task<Order> GetByIdAsync(int id)
    {
        return await _context.
Orders.FindAsync(id);
    }
```

```
    public async Task AddAsync(Order order)
    {
        await _context.Orders.AddAsync(order);
        await _context.SaveChangesAsync();
    }

    public async Task<IEnumerable
<Order>> GetAllAsync()
    {
        return await _context.
Orders.ToListAsync();
    }
}
```

- **External Services**: Implement any external services or APIs the application interacts with.

4. Implementing the User Interface Layer

4.1 Developing the UI

- **Select UI Framework**: Choose an appropriate UI framework (e.g., React, Angular, ASP.NET MVC) based on project requirements.

4.2 Creating Controllers

- **Implement MVC Controllers**: Create controllers that handle incoming requests and interact with application services.

Example: OrderController

csharp
Copy code

CHAPTER 15: IMPLEMENTING CLEAN ARCHITECTURE IN REAL-WORLD...

```
[ApiController]
[Route("api/orders")]
public class OrderController : ControllerBase
{
    private readonly PlaceOrderCommandHandler _placeOrderHandler;

    public OrderController
(PlaceOrderCommandHandler placeOrderHandler)
    {
        _placeOrderHandler = placeOrderHandler;
    }

    [HttpPost]
    public async Task<IActionResult> PlaceOrder([FromBody] PlaceOrderCommand command)
    {
        await _placeOrderHandler.Handle(command);
        return Ok();
    }
}
```

4.3 Views and User Interaction

- **Design Views**: Create views that present data to users and facilitate user interaction.

Example: Order View in Razor

```
html
Copy code
@model OrderDto

<h2>Order Details</h2>
```

```
<p>Order ID: @Model.Id</p>
<p>Order Date: @Model.OrderDate</p>
<ul>
    @foreach (var line in Model.OrderLines)
    {
        <li>@line.ProductName - Quantity: @line.Quantity</li>
    }
</ul>
```

5. Testing the Implementation

5.1 Unit Testing

- **Test the Core Layer**: Write unit tests for entities and application services.

Example: Unit Test for Order Entity

```csharp
Copy code
public class OrderTests
{
    [Fact]
    public void AddOrderLine_ShouldIncreaseOrderTotal()
    {
        // Arrange
        var order = new Order(DateTime.UtcNow);
        var product = new Product(1, "Test Product", 10.00m);

        // Act
        order.AddOrderLine(product, 2);
```

CHAPTER 15: IMPLEMENTING CLEAN ARCHITECTURE IN REAL-WORLD...

```csharp
        // Assert
        Assert.Equal(20.00m, order.Total);
    }
}
```

5.2 Integration Testing

- **Test Repository Implementations**: Write integration tests to validate the interaction with the database.

Example: Integration Test for SqlOrderRepository

```csharp
Copy code
[Fact]
public async Task Add_ShouldSaveOrderToDatabase()
{
    // Arrange
    var options = new DbContextOptionsBuilder<OrderContext>()
        .UseInMemoryDatabase("TestDatabase")
        .Options;

    using (var context =
 new OrderContext(options))
    {
        var repository = new SqlOrderRepository(context);
        var order = new Order
(DateTime.UtcNow);

        // Act
        await repository.AddAsync(order);
    }

    using (var context =
```

```
new OrderContext(options))
    {
        // Assert
        Assert.Single(await context.
Orders.ToListAsync());
    }
}
```

5.3 End-to-End Testing

- **Test User Interactions**: Implement end-to-end tests to validate the entire user journey.

Example: End-to-End Test Using Selenium

```csharp
Copy code
public class OrderEndToEndTests : IDisposable
{
    private readonly IWebDriver _driver;

    public OrderEndToEndTests()
    {
        _driver = new ChromeDriver();
    }

    [Fact]
    public async Task CreateOrder_
ShouldDisplayOrderInList()
    {
        // Arrange
        _driver.Navigate().GoToUrl("http:
//localhost:5000/Order/Create");
        // Fill in form and submit...

        // Assert
        var orderTable = _driver.
FindElement(By.Id("ordersTable"));
```

CHAPTER 15: IMPLEMENTING CLEAN ARCHITECTURE IN REAL-WORLD...

```
        Assert.Contains
("Order Total", orderTable.Text);
    }

    public void Dispose()
    {
        _driver.Quit();
    }
}
```

6. Deploying the Application

6.1 Choosing a Deployment Strategy

- **On-Premises vs. Cloud**: Evaluate whether to deploy on-premises or in the cloud based on business needs and scalability requirements.

6.2 Preparing for Deployment

- **Dockerization**: Consider containerizing the application to ensure consistency across environments.

Example: Dockerfile for ASP.NET Core Application

```dockerfile
Copy code
FROM mcr.microsoft.com/dotnet/aspnet:5.0 AS base
WORKDIR /app
EXPOSE 80

FROM mcr.microsoft.com/dotnet/sdk:5.0 AS build
WORKDIR /src
COPY ["MyApplication/MyApplication.csproj"
, "MyApplication/"]
```

```
RUN dotnet restore
"MyApplication/MyApplication.csproj"
COPY . .
WORKDIR "/src/MyApplication"
RUN dotnet build "MyApplication.csproj"
-c Release -o /app/build

FROM build AS publish
RUN dotnet publish
"MyApplication.csproj"
 -c Release -o /app/publish

FROM base AS final
WORKDIR /app
COPY --from=publish /app/publish .
ENTRYPOINT ["dotnet", "MyApplication.dll"]
```

6.3 CI/CD Pipeline Setup

- **Automate Build and Deployment**: Set up a CI/CD pipeline to automate the build and deployment process.

Example: GitHub Actions CI/CD Workflow

```yaml
Copy code
name: CI/CD

on:
  push:
    branches:
      - main

jobs:
  build:
    runs-on: ubuntu-latest

    steps:
```

```yaml
      - name: Checkout code
        uses: actions/checkout@v2

      - name: Set up .NET
        uses: actions/setup-dotnet@v1
        with:
           dotnet-version: '5.0.x'

      - name: Restore dependencies
        run: dotnet restore

      - name: Build
        run: dotnet build --configuration Release

      - name: Run tests
        run: dotnet test --configuration Release

      - name: Publish
        run: dotnet publish
   --configuration Release -o ./publish

      - name: Deploy
        run: |
          az webapp up --name
   <App-Name> --resource-group <Resource-Group>
```

7. Monitoring and Maintenance

7.1 Implementing Monitoring Solutions

- **Use APM Tools**: Implement Application Performance Monitoring (APM) tools to monitor the application in production.

Example: Using Azure Application Insights

```csharp
Copy code
services.AddApplicationInsightsTelemetry
(Configuration
["ApplicationInsights:
InstrumentationKey"]);
```

7.2 Setting Up Logging

- **Structured Logging**: Utilize structured logging to capture detailed information about application behavior.

Example: Configuring Serilog

```csharp
Copy code
Log.Logger = new LoggerConfiguration()
    .WriteTo.Console()
    .CreateLogger();
```

7.3 Regular Maintenance

- **Perform Code Reviews**: Regularly review code for adherence to Clean Architecture principles and best practices.
- **Refactor as Necessary**: Continually refactor the application to improve maintainability and performance.

8. Common Pitfalls and How to Avoid Them

8.1 Over-Engineering
Avoid over-engineering the application architecture. Stick to simplicity and implement only the necessary features.

8.2 Neglecting Documentation
Keep thorough documentation of architectural decisions, code structure, and setup processes to aid future developers.

8.3 Ignoring Performance Considerations

Regularly monitor application performance and address bottlenecks proactively.

8.4 Underestimating Security Needs

Security should be a primary concern throughout the development process. Implement security best practices from the outset.

Conclusion

In this chapter, we explored the step-by-step process of implementing Clean Architecture in real-world projects. By following best practices, understanding potential pitfalls, and utilizing a structured approach, developers can create robust, scalable, and maintainable applications.

Implementing Clean Architecture effectively allows teams to enhance collaboration, streamline development processes, and ultimately deliver high-quality software that meets user needs.

In the next chapter, we will summarize the key takeaways from the book, providing guidance for readers looking to implement Clean Architecture principles in their future projects.

Conclusion

In this concluding chapter, we will summarize the key insights and takeaways from the book, emphasizing the importance of Clean Architecture in modern software development. We will reflect on the principles, practices, and methodologies discussed throughout the chapters, providing a cohesive understanding of how to implement Clean Architecture effectively in real-world projects.

1. The Importance of Clean Architecture

Clean Architecture is more than just a design pattern; it represents a philosophy of software development that prioritizes maintainability, testability, and scalability. By emphasizing the separation of concerns, Clean Architecture enables developers to create systems that are robust and adaptable to changing requirements.

- **Separation of Concerns**: This principle allows different parts of the application to be developed, tested, and maintained independently. This modularity not only facilitates easier updates but also enhances collaboration among team members with different areas of expertise.
- **Testability**: Clean Architecture promotes writing unit and integration tests by decoupling components. This means developers can verify the functionality of individual units without relying on the entire system, leading to higher code quality and reduced regression issues.
- **Scalability**: As applications grow, Clean Architecture allows teams to

add features and make changes without overhauling the entire system. The architecture can support scaling efforts, whether by introducing new services in a microservices approach or enhancing existing ones.

2. Core Principles Recap

Throughout the book, we have delved into the core principles that underpin Clean Architecture:

- **Independence from Frameworks**: The architecture is not tied to specific frameworks or technologies, allowing flexibility in choosing the right tools for the job.
- **UI Independence**: The user interface can be altered or replaced without affecting the underlying business logic, facilitating design updates and technology shifts.
- **Test-Driven Development (TDD)**: Embracing TDD ensures that testing is an integral part of the development process, leading to higher-quality code and reduced bugs.

3. Implementation Strategies

We explored various strategies for implementing Clean Architecture in real-world projects:

- **Project Structuring**: A well-defined folder structure helps maintain clarity and organization within the application. Following conventions makes it easier for developers to navigate the codebase.
- **Layered Architecture**: By implementing distinct layers—Core, Application, Infrastructure, and UI—we can ensure that each layer has its responsibilities, leading to a more organized and maintainable codebase.
- **Use of Modern Technologies**: The integration of modern frameworks, libraries, and tools enhances development speed and efficiency. For example, using Entity Framework for data access or ASP.NET Core for building APIs streamlines common tasks.

4. Challenges and Solutions

While implementing Clean Architecture, developers may encounter various challenges:

- **Complexity**: The initial setup of Clean Architecture may seem complex, especially for smaller projects. However, adopting these principles from the start prepares the application for future growth.
- **Performance Concerns**: Optimizing performance while maintaining the benefits of Clean Architecture is crucial. Implementing caching strategies, optimizing queries, and leveraging asynchronous programming can help mitigate performance issues.
- **Cultural Shifts**: Transitioning to Clean Architecture may require a cultural shift within an organization. It is essential to foster collaboration among team members, encourage continuous learning, and ensure that everyone is aligned with architectural principles.

5. Future Trends and Adaptability

The book also highlighted the importance of staying current with emerging trends that impact software development:

- **Microservices and Serverless Architectures**: These trends provide flexibility and scalability, aligning well with Clean Architecture principles. By breaking applications into smaller, independent services, developers can respond more quickly to changes in user requirements.
- **Domain-Driven Design (DDD)**: DDD complements Clean Architecture by emphasizing the importance of understanding the domain and fostering collaboration between technical and domain experts.
- **Event-Driven Architectures**: As applications become more interactive, adopting event-driven designs can enhance responsiveness and decouple components.
- **CI/CD Practices**: Implementing CI/CD pipelines automates testing and deployment processes, ensuring that applications are released faster and with higher quality.

6. Key Takeaways

To conclude, here are the key takeaways from the book:

- Clean Architecture provides a structured approach to software design that enhances maintainability, testability, and scalability.
- The principles of Clean Architecture—such as separation of concerns and framework independence—are essential for building robust applications.
- Implementing Clean Architecture requires careful planning, a clear understanding of project requirements, and a commitment to best practices.
- Continuous learning and adaptation to emerging technologies and trends are crucial for developers looking to maintain a competitive edge.

7. Encouragement for Practitioners

For developers, architects, and teams adopting Clean Architecture, it is essential to embrace the journey of continuous improvement. The software landscape is ever-evolving, and the ability to adapt to new challenges and technologies will empower you to create exceptional software that meets user needs.

Remember that the goal of Clean Architecture is not just to impose structure on your codebase but to create an environment where high-quality software can flourish. Embrace the principles and practices discussed in this book, and you'll be well on your way to building successful applications that stand the test of time.

www.ingramcontent.com/pod-product-compliance
Lightning Source LLC
Chambersburg PA
CBHW071023240526
45469CB00006BD/2063